# HOW IT WORKS

# THE WORLD OF
# INSECT LIFE

Gerald Legg and Steve Weston

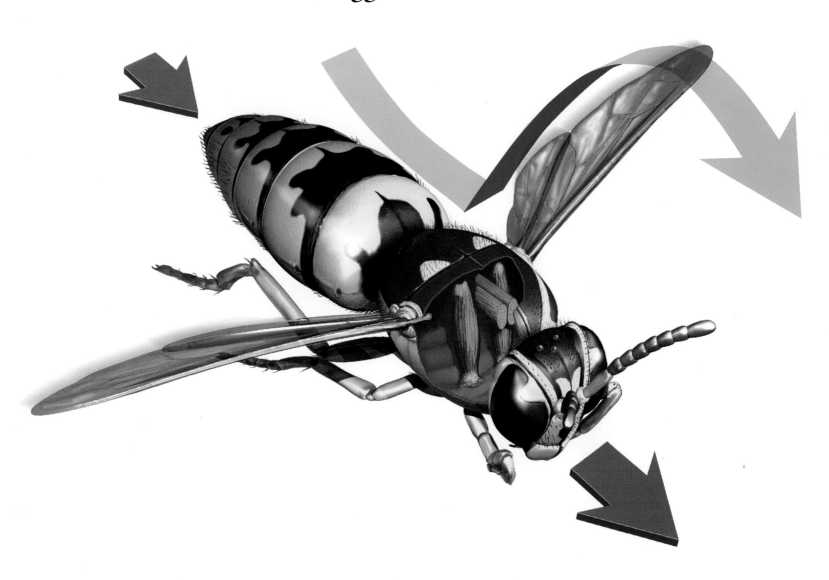

**HORUS EDITIONS**

**Published by Horus Editions**
**Award Publications Limited,**
**1st Floor, 27 Longford Street,**
**London NW1 3DZ**

**Copyright © 2000 Horus Editions**

Series editor Elizabeth Miles
Designed by Steve Weston, Richard Rowan
Illustrations by Steve Weston
Additional illustrations by Ruth Lindsay, Jim Channell

ISBN 1-899762-49-3 (Cased)
ISBN 1-899762-51-5 (Paperback)

Printed in Singapore

# HOW IT WORKS

# CONTENTS

| | | | |
|---|---|---|---|
| What is an Insect? | 6 | Ants' Nest | 32 |
| Armour Plating | 8 | Bees' Nest | 34 |
| Insect Eyes | 10 | Rainforest Life | 36 |
| Feelers | 12 | Insects in Water | 38 |
| Flying | 14 | Woodland Life | 40 |
| Hunting | 16 | Desert Insects | 42 |
| Self-defence | 18 | Microscopic Life | 44 |
| Colour and Shape | 20 | Index | 46 |
| Feeding | 22 | | |
| Parasites | 24 | | |
| Mating | 26 | | |
| New Life | 28 | | |
| Changing Shape | 30 | | |

# What is an Insect?

THERE are more insects on Earth than any other type of creature. Insects are strong and small, with three pairs of legs but no backbone. Like knights in armour, they have a tough outer covering. This outer skeleton (exoskeleton) supports and protects the insect's body parts and soft insides.

The protected head of an insect holds the brain and carries the antennae, eyes, mouth, and special jaws. Different insects have different shaped jaws, allowing them to eat all kinds of things. The abdomen contains the main organs, including those for digesting food. Throughout the body, special breathing tubes called trachea carry gases to and from the body's tissues. A long thin heart circulates blood. A nerve cord that controls various body processes runs from the brain to the tip of the abdomen.

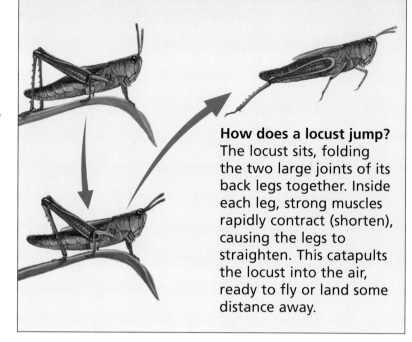

**How does a locust jump?** The locust sits, folding the two large joints of its back legs together. Inside each leg, strong muscles rapidly contract (shorten), causing the legs to straighten. This catapults the locust into the air, ready to fly or land some distance away.

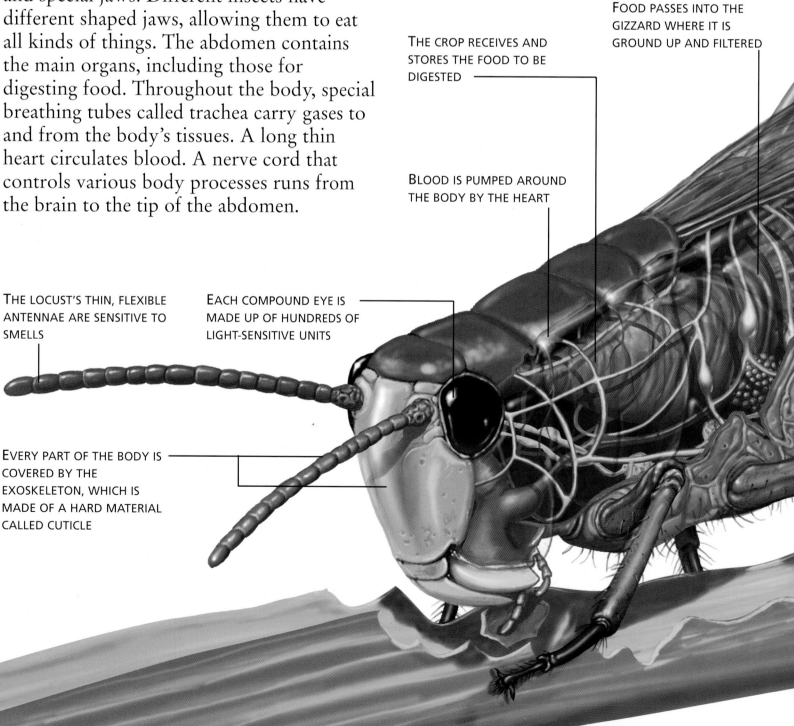

THE CROP RECEIVES AND STORES THE FOOD TO BE DIGESTED

FOOD PASSES INTO THE GIZZARD WHERE IT IS GROUND UP AND FILTERED

BLOOD IS PUMPED AROUND THE BODY BY THE HEART

THE LOCUST'S THIN, FLEXIBLE ANTENNAE ARE SENSITIVE TO SMELLS

EACH COMPOUND EYE IS MADE UP OF HUNDREDS OF LIGHT-SENSITIVE UNITS

EVERY PART OF THE BODY IS COVERED BY THE EXOSKELETON, WHICH IS MADE OF A HARD MATERIAL CALLED CUTICLE

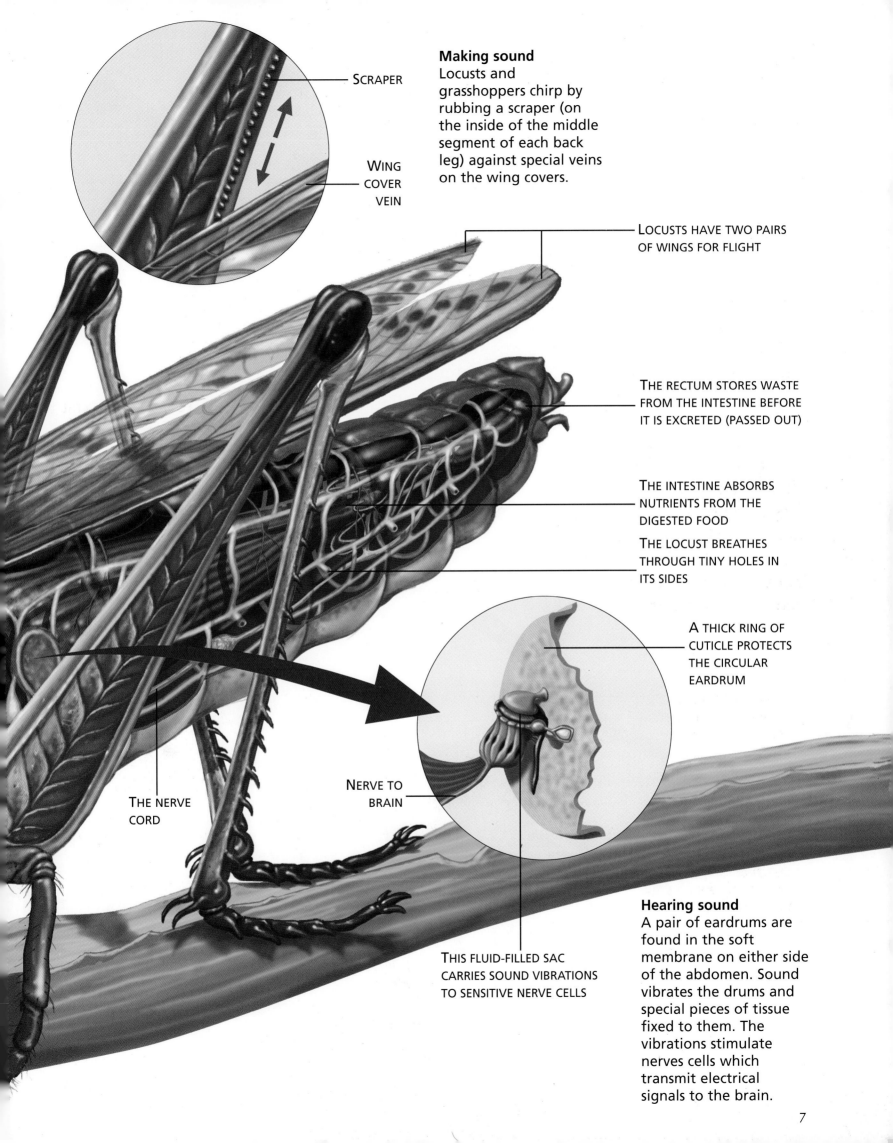

SCRAPER

WING COVER VEIN

**Making sound**
Locusts and grasshoppers chirp by rubbing a scraper (on the inside of the middle segment of each back leg) against special veins on the wing covers.

LOCUSTS HAVE TWO PAIRS OF WINGS FOR FLIGHT

THE RECTUM STORES WASTE FROM THE INTESTINE BEFORE IT IS EXCRETED (PASSED OUT)

THE INTESTINE ABSORBS NUTRIENTS FROM THE DIGESTED FOOD

THE LOCUST BREATHES THROUGH TINY HOLES IN ITS SIDES

A THICK RING OF CUTICLE PROTECTS THE CIRCULAR EARDRUM

NERVE TO BRAIN

THE NERVE CORD

THIS FLUID-FILLED SAC CARRIES SOUND VIBRATIONS TO SENSITIVE NERVE CELLS

**Hearing sound**
A pair of eardrums are found in the soft membrane on either side of the abdomen. Sound vibrates the drums and special pieces of tissue fixed to them. The vibrations stimulate nerves cells which transmit electrical signals to the brain.

# Armour Plating

INSECTS WEAR their skeleton on the outside, like armour. Out of all the types of animals in the world, insects have been more able to survive because of this amazing exoskeleton. It is made of a tough, skin-like substance, called cuticle, which protects the organs and supports the muscles. Insects' jaws are covered in very hard cuticle, whereas at the joints it is soft and flexible. Thin tubes of cuticle make strong jointed legs. Both the head and thorax are like boxes made of thick cuticle. The head protects the brain and carries the sense organs and mouth parts. The strong thorax supports the wing and leg muscles. In contrast, the abdomen which holds most of the body organs is flexible and made of several rings of cuticle, called segments.

**Beetle**
There are over 330,000 species of beetle ranging in size from 0.5 mm to over 155 mm. They are found everywhere. Hard, tough forewings protect their delicate flying wings. Shown here, is a scarab beetle.

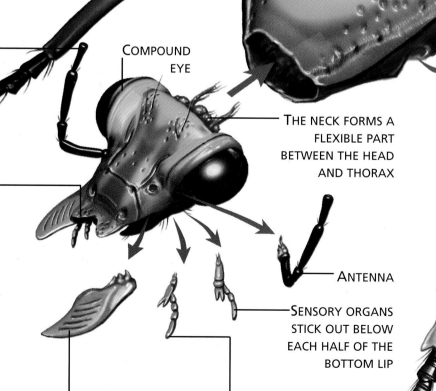

THE THORAX IS PACKED WITH MUSCLES TO DRIVE THE WINGS AND LEGS

EACH MULTI-JOINTED, FLEXIBLE ANTENNA IS COVERED IN SENSE CELLS TO DETECT SMELLS IN THE AIR

COMPOUND EYE

THE NECK FORMS A FLEXIBLE PART BETWEEN THE HEAD AND THORAX

MUSCLES OF THE UPPER LEG JOINT ARE FIXED TO THE THORAX

THE TOP LIP IS HINGED TO THE FRONT OF THE FACE SO THAT IT CAN MOVE

ANTENNA

**Insect head**
The head carries the main sense organs – this beetle has a pair of compound eyes, simple eyes, and antennae. At the front of the mouth there are three sets of mouthparts: the mandibles (jaws), maxillae, and bottom lip. A top lip covers the mandibles. The head is attached to the thorax by a narrow, flexible neck.

SENSORY ORGANS STICK OUT BELOW EACH HALF OF THE BOTTOM LIP

INSECTS HAVE THREE PAIRS OF LEGS

MANDIBLE: A SHARP JAW FOR CUTTING FOOD AND FIGHTING

MAXILLA: A SMALL JAW WITH SENSORY ORGANS THAT HELPS CUT UP FOOD

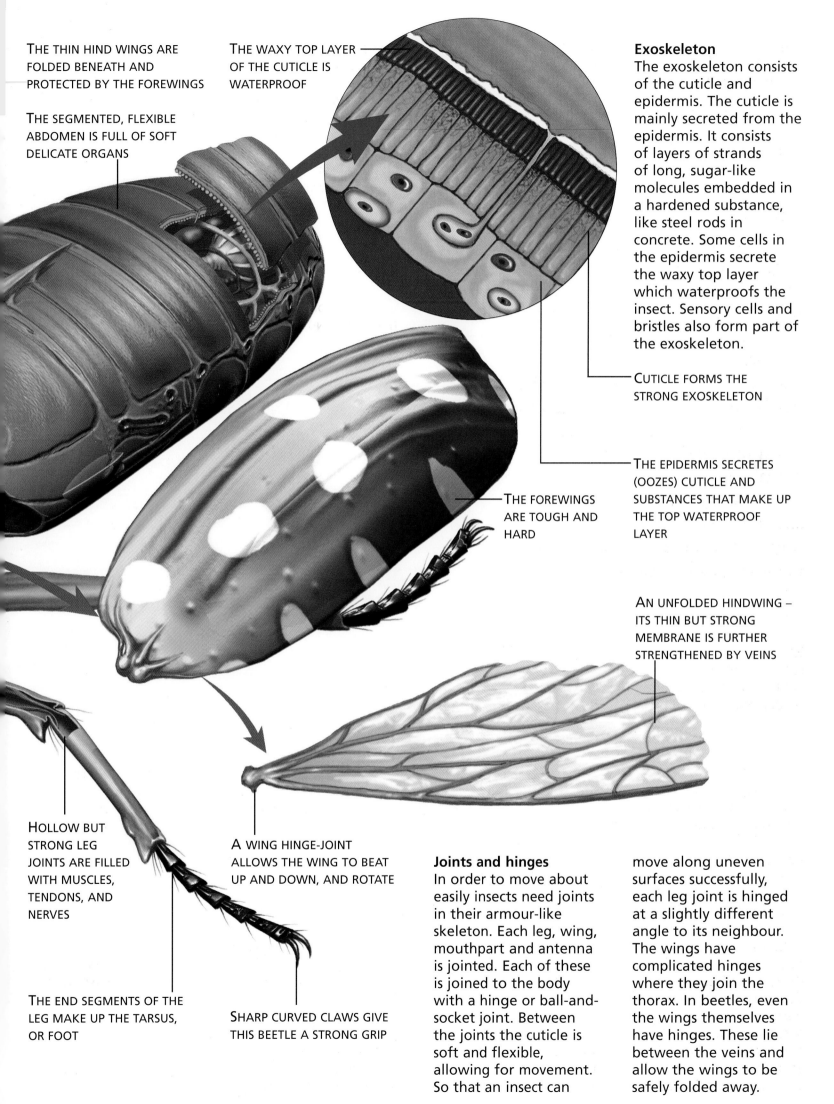

THE THIN HIND WINGS ARE FOLDED BENEATH AND PROTECTED BY THE FOREWINGS

THE SEGMENTED, FLEXIBLE ABDOMEN IS FULL OF SOFT DELICATE ORGANS

THE WAXY TOP LAYER OF THE CUTICLE IS WATERPROOF

## Exoskeleton

The exoskeleton consists of the cuticle and epidermis. The cuticle is mainly secreted from the epidermis. It consists of layers of strands of long, sugar-like molecules embedded in a hardened substance, like steel rods in concrete. Some cells in the epidermis secrete the waxy top layer which waterproofs the insect. Sensory cells and bristles also form part of the exoskeleton.

CUTICLE FORMS THE STRONG EXOSKELETON

THE FOREWINGS ARE TOUGH AND HARD

THE EPIDERMIS SECRETES (OOZES) CUTICLE AND SUBSTANCES THAT MAKE UP THE TOP WATERPROOF LAYER

AN UNFOLDED HINDWING – ITS THIN BUT STRONG MEMBRANE IS FURTHER STRENGTHENED BY VEINS

HOLLOW BUT STRONG LEG JOINTS ARE FILLED WITH MUSCLES, TENDONS, AND NERVES

A WING HINGE-JOINT ALLOWS THE WING TO BEAT UP AND DOWN, AND ROTATE

THE END SEGMENTS OF THE LEG MAKE UP THE TARSUS, OR FOOT

SHARP CURVED CLAWS GIVE THIS BEETLE A STRONG GRIP

## Joints and hinges

In order to move about easily insects need joints in their armour-like skeleton. Each leg, wing, mouthpart and antenna is jointed. Each of these is joined to the body with a hinge or ball-and-socket joint. Between the joints the cuticle is soft and flexible, allowing for movement. So that an insect can move along uneven surfaces successfully, each leg joint is hinged at a slightly different angle to its neighbour. The wings have complicated hinges where they join the thorax. In beetles, even the wings themselves have hinges. These lie between the veins and allow the wings to be safely folded away.

# Insect Eyes

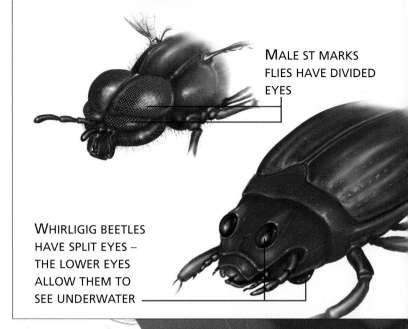

MALE ST MARKS FLIES HAVE DIVIDED EYES

WHIRLIGIG BEETLES HAVE SPLIT EYES – THE LOWER EYES ALLOW THEM TO SEE UNDERWATER

INSECTS HAVE two types of eyes. The largest are the compound eyes, which are covered with a honeycomb pattern of hexagons. Each hexagon is the transparent cuticle of an individual organ of sight. Insects can have as many as 30,000 hexagonal shapes in each compound eye or as few as one. Each of these sight organs (called ommatidia) sees only a tiny part of the surroundings. But by joining these parts together in the brain, the insect is able to see a full image.

The second type of eyes, called ocelli, are usually much smaller. They are similar to human eyes, but cannot see an image. Instead they are very sensitive to light. Nocturnal insects, which are active at night, have very large ocelli.

**Ommatidia**

Light from the outside world enters each ommatidium and is focused by a hexagonal lens. It then passes through the crystal-like cone which also helps to focus it. Next, it reaches the nerve cells which have a light-sensitive inner part (called the rhabdom). From here the light is carried by nerve fibres to the brain. Pigment cells surround the nerve cells and stop light leaking into the rest of the eye, as this would spoil the image.

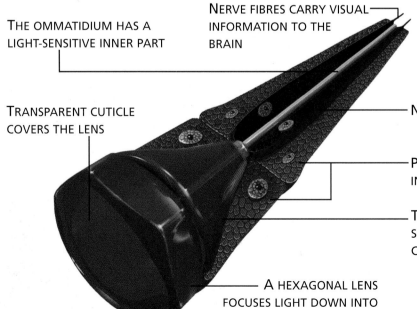

THE OMMATIDIUM HAS A LIGHT-SENSITIVE INNER PART

NERVE FIBRES CARRY VISUAL INFORMATION TO THE BRAIN

TRANSPARENT CUTICLE COVERS THE LENS

NERVE CELL

PIGMENT CELLS KEEP LIGHT INSIDE THE OMMATIDIUM

THE CRYSTAL-LIKE CONE IS SURROUNDED BY PIGMENT CELLS

A HEXAGONAL LENS FOCUSES LIGHT DOWN INTO THE OMMATIDIUM

**Unusual eyes**

Whirligig beetles live on the surface of ponds. Their eyes are split, with one pair on top and the other underneath. This lets them see above and below the water surface at the same time. The eyes of male St Marks flies are divided into an upper part with large ommatidia, and a lower part with small ommatidia.

**Damselfly**

Damselflies are delicate but agile hunters. Large compound eyes (1) provide all-round and very clear vision. Light-sensitive ommatidia (2) send their mass of signals down the huge optic nerves (3) to the brain (4), which analyses information from all the senses. The damselfly's three small ocelli (5) are sensitive to light intensity. They are situated between the widely spaced compound eyes.

THE TWO SHORT ANTENNAE CAN SENSE SMELLS

THE SHIMMERING, COLOURFUL COMPOUND EYES ARE MADE UP OF THOUSANDS OF HEXAGONAL LENSES

WIDELY SPACED EYES MAKE IT EASIER TO JUDGE DISTANCES

THE ENDS OF THE OMMATIDIA ARE CONNECTED TO THE OPTIC NERVES INSIDE THE FLY'S HEAD

MOUTH PARTS FOR EATING PREY

**Invisible colour**

Many insects can see ultraviolet, a colour invisible to us. Some flowers reflect this colour so that insects can see special markings that will guide them to the flower's nectaries.

11

# Feelers

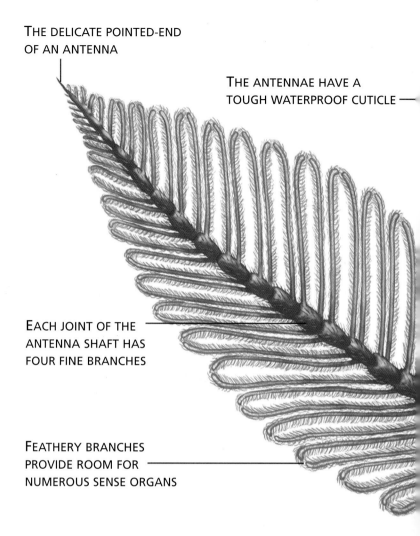

THE DELICATE POINTED-END OF AN ANTENNA

THE ANTENNAE HAVE A TOUGH WATERPROOF CUTICLE

EACH JOINT OF THE ANTENNA SHAFT HAS FOUR FINE BRANCHES

FEATHERY BRANCHES PROVIDE ROOM FOR NUMEROUS SENSE ORGANS

INSECT FEELERS are remarkable instruments. The two feelers (antennae) are covered in many thousands of sensory cells, which can detect tiny amounts of chemicals, even a single molecule. This means, for example, that a male moth can detect the scent of a female moth that is over a kilometre away. Insects can even 'see' using their feelers, mapping out the shape of their surroundings from the smells in it. Insects use sensory cells to find their way about and to find many other things – a mate, the right plant on which to lay their eggs, tasty prey or a good host to live on. Although insects have other chemical-sensitive organs, such as taste organs, these are not as sensitive and need direct contact with a substance.

THE LEGS AND BODY ARE COVERED IN A THICK MASS OF 'HAIRS' WHICH MAKES FOR SILENT FLIGHT

LARGE EYES FOR SEEING IN MOON LIGHT

EMPEROR MOTHS INCLUDE THE LARGEST MOTHS – SOME HAVE A WINGSPAN OF UP TO 30 CENTIMETRES

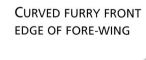

① ② ③ ④ ⑤ ⑥ ⑦

CURVED FURRY FRONT EDGE OF FORE-WING

### Types of feelers

Feelers come in a great variety of shapes and sizes, especially in the beetle world. Springtails and dragonflies have thread-like feelers (1). Some ground beetles have a saw-edge variety (2). Termites and earwigs have bead-like ones (3) and those of burying beetles are clubbed (4). Sawflies and cardinal beetles have feather-like feelers (5) and the cockchafer beetle and june bug have feather-tipped ones (6). Weevils and parastic wasps have flexible 'elbowed' feelers (7).

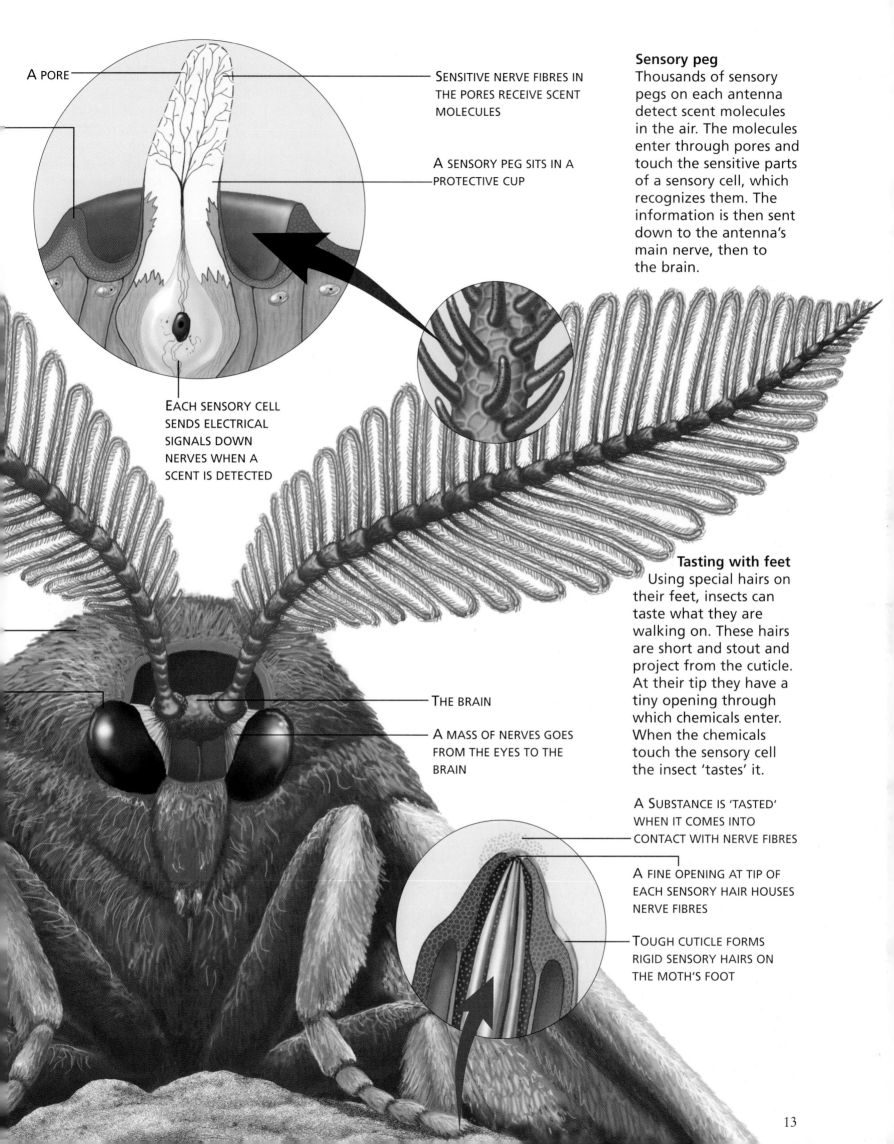

A PORE

SENSITIVE NERVE FIBRES IN THE PORES RECEIVE SCENT MOLECULES

A SENSORY PEG SITS IN A PROTECTIVE CUP

EACH SENSORY CELL SENDS ELECTRICAL SIGNALS DOWN NERVES WHEN A SCENT IS DETECTED

## Sensory peg

Thousands of sensory pegs on each antenna detect scent molecules in the air. The molecules enter through pores and touch the sensitive parts of a sensory cell, which recognizes them. The information is then sent down to the antenna's main nerve, then to the brain.

THE BRAIN

A MASS OF NERVES GOES FROM THE EYES TO THE BRAIN

## Tasting with feet

Using special hairs on their feet, insects can taste what they are walking on. These hairs are short and stout and project from the cuticle. At their tip they have a tiny opening through which chemicals enter. When the chemicals touch the sensory cell the insect 'tastes' it.

A SUBSTANCE IS 'TASTED' WHEN IT COMES INTO CONTACT WITH NERVE FIBRES

A FINE OPENING AT TIP OF EACH SENSORY HAIR HOUSES NERVE FIBRES

TOUGH CUTICLE FORMS RIGID SENSORY HAIRS ON THE MOTH'S FOOT

13

# Flying

INSECTS CAN do just about any flying manoeuvre. They can fly forward, backward, sideways, or upside down; they can loop, hover, swoop, and even do vertical take-offs. An insect's thorax is an extremely complicated, tough but flexible, powerhouse – packed with muscles that control the movement of the wings. Each wing is hinged to the thorax by ball-and-socket joints that pivot near the inner end of the wing. When the wing moves it rocks on these joints like a seesaw that can swivel round in all directions. To move their wings some insects, including dragonflies, use muscles fixed directly to the end of the wings. Most other insects use muscles that are fixed to the top and bottom and the front and back of the thorax.

AS THE WASP MOVES FORWARDS AND LIFTS INTO THE AIR, ITS WINGS ROTATE UP AND DOWN

**Linked pairs**
Wings that are linked together make for efficient flight. Butterflies link their wings by overlapping them, and wasps have hooks on their hind-wing that catch into a fold on the fore-wing.

EACH PAIR OF WINGS IS LINKED TOGETHER, GIVING EXTRA LIFT

THE WING TILTS WITH THE LEADING EDGE FACING DOWNWARDS

VEINS GIVE THE WING STRENGTH AND SHAPE FOR EFFICIENT FLIGHT

**Wing down**
Many insects, like this wasp, move their wings down by contracting (shortening) the thorax muscles that run front-to-back and relaxing (lengthening) those that run top-to-bottom. This makes the thorax bulge. The thorax cuticle (outer covering) is like tough elastic, so when it bulges, the wings, which pivot like a seesaw, are flicked down.

ON THE UP STROKE, THE WING TILTS UPWARDS

**Wing types**
The dragonfly (1) has two pairs of wings that move alternately. They are driven by muscles fixed directly to the wings. A butterfly (2) has slow-beating wings that overlap – the front wing pulls the back one down. Flies (3) use one pair of wings for flying, and a second pair form special organs for controlling flight. Beetles (4) have tough front wings that protect the delicate hind-wings when they are folded away.

14

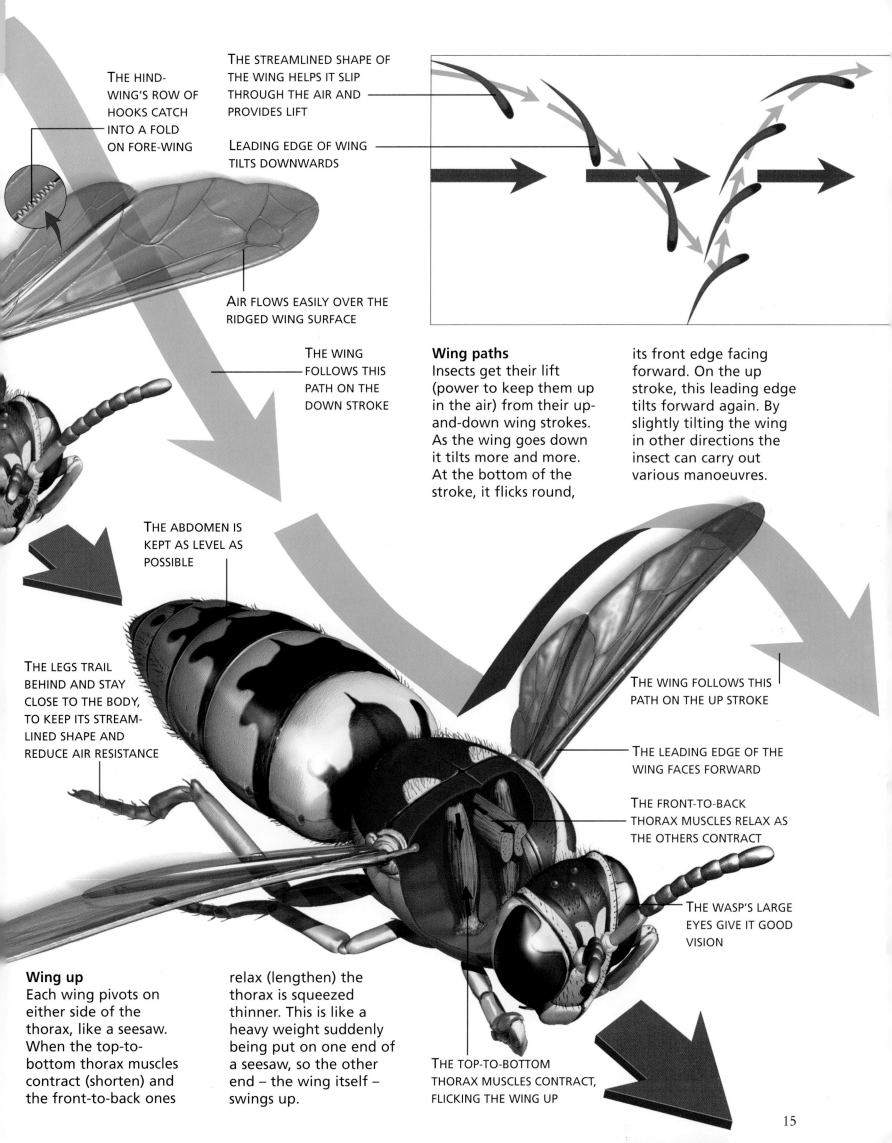

THE HIND-WING'S ROW OF HOOKS CATCH INTO A FOLD ON FORE-WING

THE STREAMLINED SHAPE OF THE WING HELPS IT SLIP THROUGH THE AIR AND PROVIDES LIFT

LEADING EDGE OF WING TILTS DOWNWARDS

AIR FLOWS EASILY OVER THE RIDGED WING SURFACE

THE WING FOLLOWS THIS PATH ON THE DOWN STROKE

THE ABDOMEN IS KEPT AS LEVEL AS POSSIBLE

THE LEGS TRAIL BEHIND AND STAY CLOSE TO THE BODY, TO KEEP ITS STREAMLINED SHAPE AND REDUCE AIR RESISTANCE

THE WING FOLLOWS THIS PATH ON THE UP STROKE

THE LEADING EDGE OF THE WING FACES FORWARD

THE FRONT-TO-BACK THORAX MUSCLES RELAX AS THE OTHERS CONTRACT

THE WASP'S LARGE EYES GIVE IT GOOD VISION

THE TOP-TO-BOTTOM THORAX MUSCLES CONTRACT, FLICKING THE WING UP

## Wing paths

Insects get their lift (power to keep them up in the air) from their up-and-down wing strokes. As the wing goes down it tilts more and more. At the bottom of the stroke, it flicks round, its front edge facing forward. On the up stroke, this leading edge tilts forward again. By slightly tilting the wing in other directions the insect can carry out various manoeuvres.

## Wing up

Each wing pivots on either side of the thorax, like a seesaw. When the top-to-bottom thorax muscles contract (shorten) and the front-to-back ones relax (lengthen) the thorax is squeezed thinner. This is like a heavy weight suddenly being put on one end of a seesaw, so the other end – the wing itself – swings up.

# Hunting

PREDATORS need quick reactions and speed to catch more wary and fast-moving prey. They are armed with powerful jaws, designed to capture, kill, and cut up their meal. Praying mantids (*right*) use their special front legs to catch their victims, before biting the prey to pieces with their jaws. Many insects are active hunters, prowling around looking for suitable prey. Others, such as mantids, employ a wait-and-see method. They patiently keep still until their victim comes within range, and then pounce on it. Such ambush hunters are well-camouflaged to avoid being spotted by their victims until it is too late.

**Wait and see**
A praying mantis keeps perfectly still, close to somewhere that its prey is likely to land. Its legs are bent, ready to pounce.

THE MANTIS'S EYES ARE FIXED ON ITS PREY

BALANCED ON ITS HIND LEGS, THE MANTIS IS READY TO POUNCE

THE LEAF PERCH HELPS AS CAMOUFLAGE

THE MIDDLE AND REAR LEGS ARE CLOSE TOGETHER AND USED IN WALKING

THE MANTIS'S LONG THIN BODY AND WINGS RESEMBLE A PLANT

**In for the kill**
The patience of the praying mantis is rewarded. With its keen vision the praying mantis spots a bee landing on a flower. Using its claws, the mantis firmly grips its perch. Then, in the blink of an eye, its powerful back legs catapult its body forwards. At the same time, it shoots out its front legs and grabs the helpless victim, which has no time to avoid the unexpected, deadly lunge.

LONG THIN BACK AND MIDDLE LEGS ARE TYPICAL OF AN INSECT

THE MANTIS USES THE ANGLE OF ITS LEGS AND HEAD FOR A PRECISE AIM

THE STRONG CLAWS KEEP A FIRM GRIP

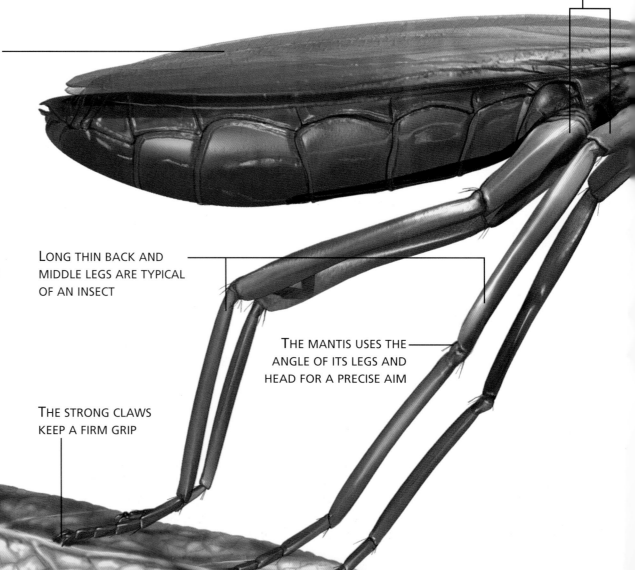

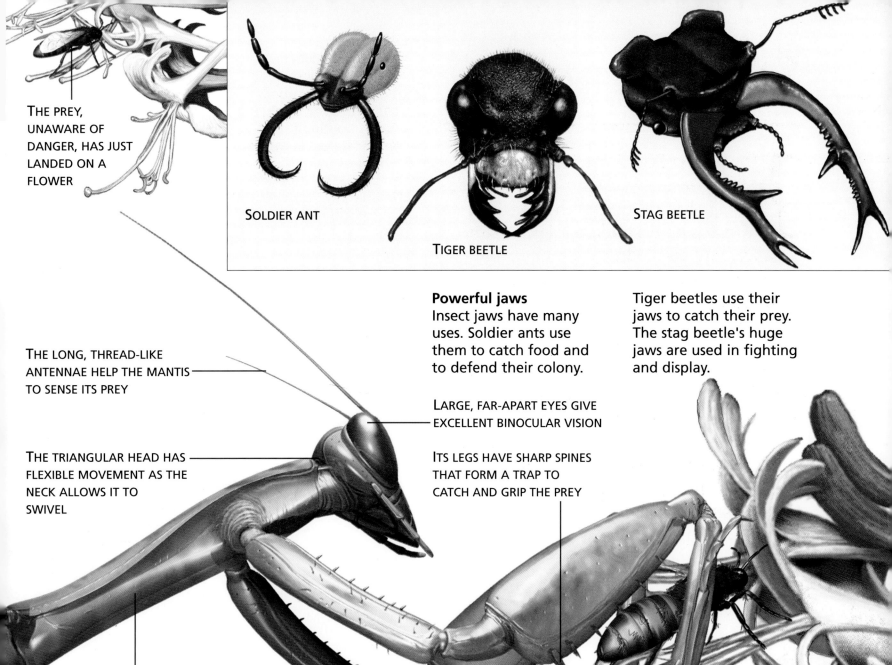

THE PREY, UNAWARE OF DANGER, HAS JUST LANDED ON A FLOWER

SOLDIER ANT

TIGER BEETLE

STAG BEETLE

THE LONG, THREAD-LIKE ANTENNAE HELP THE MANTIS TO SENSE ITS PREY

THE TRIANGULAR HEAD HAS FLEXIBLE MOVEMENT AS THE NECK ALLOWS IT TO SWIVEL

**Powerful jaws**
Insect jaws have many uses. Soldier ants use them to catch food and to defend their colony.

Tiger beetles use their jaws to catch their prey. The stag beetle's huge jaws are used in fighting and display.

LARGE, FAR-APART EYES GIVE EXCELLENT BINOCULAR VISION

ITS LEGS HAVE SHARP SPINES THAT FORM A TRAP TO CATCH AND GRIP THE PREY

THE THORAX IS LONG AND THIN

THE FRONT LEGS ARE NOT USED FOR WALKING

A LARGE CLAW FORMS PART OF THE TRAP

THE LEG MUSCLES LIE INSIDE THE LEG

**Face-to-face**
Large eyes high on a triangular head give the mantis excellent binocular (two-eyed) vision, so it can accurately judge distances. The mantis's neck enables it to swivel its head to almost any angle. Sense organs on its neck and legs also enable it to determine exactly where to strike. Gripped in the mantis's spiny legs, the victim is quickly passed to its mouth and sliced up by the mandibles.

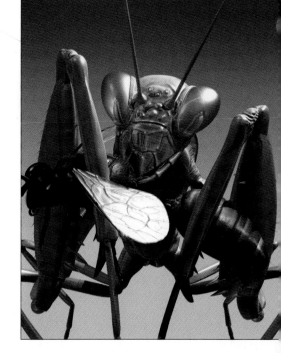

**Leg muscles**
Strong leg muscles enable the mantis to keep perfectly still until it needs to move forward to catch its meal. Then the leg muscles rapidly

straighten. The mantis's long body allows it to reach prey that is some distance away without having to walk or run up to it, which could give the prey time to escape.

17

# Self-defence

**M**ANY ANIMALS look at insects as a tasty meal, so insects have to defend themselves. Some try to avoid their enemies, by using camouflage, hiding, or running or flying away. Some face their predators. They may have amour that protects them – a thick cuticle, a coat of spines, or poisonous hairs. Or they may be more active in their defence, with strong jaws to bite and stab, a painful (even deadly) sting, or the ability to produce a strong smell or loud noise that will drive an opponent away. Some even secrete poisonous fluids or, like the bombardier beetle (*right*), spray hot irritating chemicals. Most of these masters of chemical warfare are brightly coloured so predators know to leave them alone.

### Bombardier beetle
Being a predator, the bombardier beetle is built for speed. When it is not hunting it lives under stones at the edges of fields. If disturbed or threatened in any way, it is well able to defend itself.

WITH ITS LONG ANTENNAE THE BOMBARDIER CAN SEARCH OUT PREY

THE BEETLE'S LARGE EYES ARE TYPICAL OF AN ACTIVE PREDATOR

BRIGHTLY COLOURED MARKINGS WARN PREDATORS THAT THE BEETLE CAN FIGHT BACK

LONG LEGS ENABLE THE BEETLE TO RUN FAST

### Methods of defence
Female bees (1) are armed with a sting. Glands in the bees produce a cocktail of irritating chemicals which can be pumped into a victim through a sharp needle-like lance. Many moth caterpillars (2) are covered in spines or fine hairs, which serve as protection. The hairs are sharp and break off easily, causing intense irritation in the mouth of any predator. Some termite soldiers (3) squirt glue at predators to defend their colony. Instead of biting, they spray a sticky substance from their glands, which entangles their enemy's legs and antennae. This leaf beetle (4) exudes an unpleasant drop of blood from its mouth when it is alarmed, which frightens birds, its main predator. When pursued by a bat (5) some moths emit squeaks and clicks. A bat uses sound (echolocation) to find its prey in the dark, and the moth's noises confuse its hearing, which gives the moth a chance to escape.

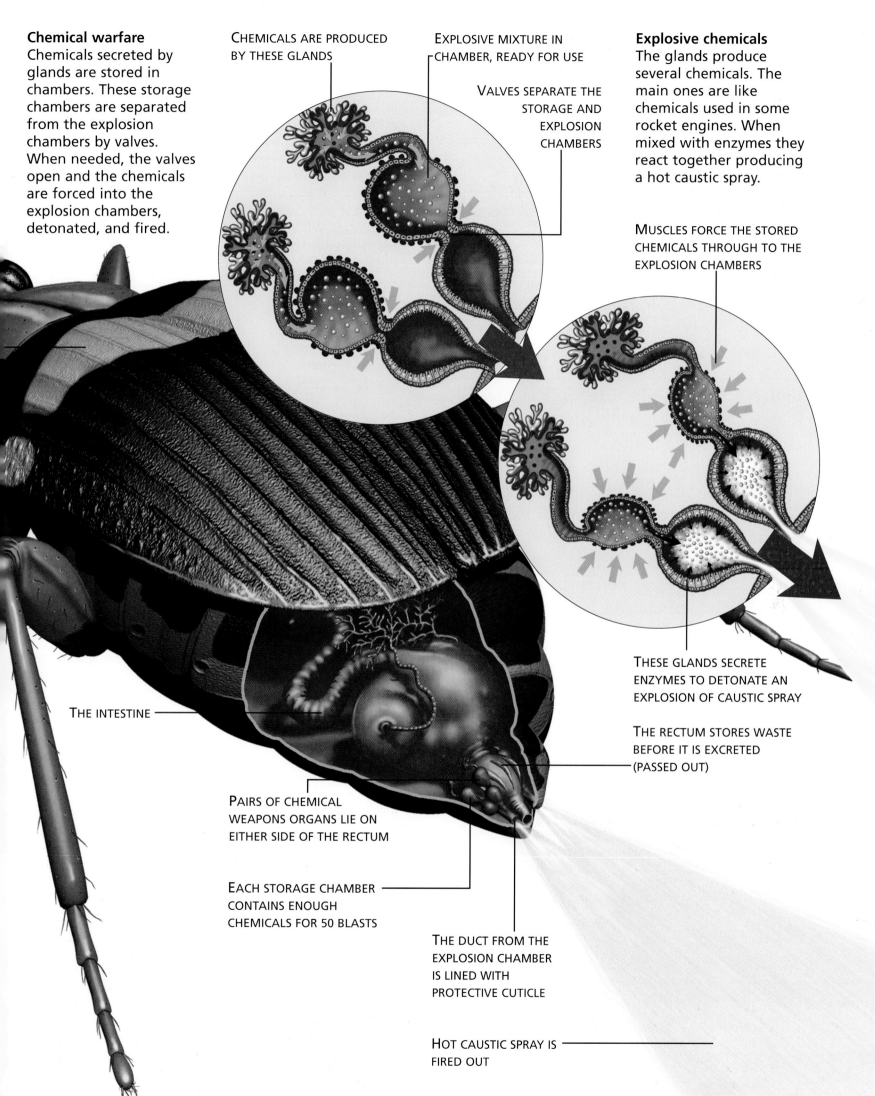

**Chemical warfare**
Chemicals secreted by glands are stored in chambers. These storage chambers are separated from the explosion chambers by valves. When needed, the valves open and the chemicals are forced into the explosion chambers, detonated, and fired.

CHEMICALS ARE PRODUCED BY THESE GLANDS

EXPLOSIVE MIXTURE IN CHAMBER, READY FOR USE

VALVES SEPARATE THE STORAGE AND EXPLOSION CHAMBERS

**Explosive chemicals**
The glands produce several chemicals. The main ones are like chemicals used in some rocket engines. When mixed with enzymes they react together producing a hot caustic spray.

MUSCLES FORCE THE STORED CHEMICALS THROUGH TO THE EXPLOSION CHAMBERS

THESE GLANDS SECRETE ENZYMES TO DETONATE AN EXPLOSION OF CAUSTIC SPRAY

THE RECTUM STORES WASTE BEFORE IT IS EXCRETED (PASSED OUT)

THE INTESTINE

PAIRS OF CHEMICAL WEAPONS ORGANS LIE ON EITHER SIDE OF THE RECTUM

EACH STORAGE CHAMBER CONTAINS ENOUGH CHEMICALS FOR 50 BLASTS

THE DUCT FROM THE EXPLOSION CHAMBER IS LINED WITH PROTECTIVE CUTICLE

HOT CAUSTIC SPRAY IS FIRED OUT

# Colour and Shape

INSECTS ARE designed for survival. They come in an infinite variety of colours and shapes which help them avoid their predators. The folded wings of many butterflies are beautifully camouflaged, blending in with surrounding leaves, lichens, or tree bark. When open, the wings may use colour in a different way. Vivid eye-spot markings can startle a predatory bird. Bright yellows and reds on black can signal to predators that the butterfly tastes nasty, warning them to leave it alone. So, an insect's cuticle (outer covering) can be used for disguise or, like a flag, as a signal to other animals. The colours and patterns can be produced with pigments (colouring in the wing tissue) and by the cuticle itself. White, blues, and greens are made by the shape of the surface of the cuticle. The varying combinations of pigment and cuticle give insects their distinctive shields of colour.

## Morpho butterfly

Morpho butterflies flash blue as they fly through the sun-dappled South American rainforests, alternately exposing their colourful upper and camouflaged lower wing surfaces. The flashing attracts other morphos and confuses predators. When they are still, with their wings folded, eye spots on the wings' undersides can startle predators.

THE WINGS' UNDERSIDES ARE CAMOUFLAGED TO RESEMBLE DEAD LEAVES

EYE-SPOTS STARTLE PREDATORS

WHITE LIGHT SHINES ONTO THE SURFACE OF THE SCALES

DIFFERENT COLOURED LIGHT IS REFLECTED FROM THE RIDGES ACCORDING TO THEIR DEPTH

THIS BEETLE HAS GOLD CAMOUFLAGE BECAUSE IT LIVES ON YELLOW FLOWERS

## Glistening like gold

Many beetles, like this gold beetle, look as though they are made of metal. They owe their metallic colouring to light reflecting back off the different layers of their semi-transparent outer cuticle (1). Below this is a softer cuticle (2), beneath which is a layer of cells, glands, and nerves (3).

THE WING OF A BUTTERFLY IS
COVERED WITH TINY
OVERLAPPING SCALES

AROUND 7000 OF THESE
TINY SCALES WOULD COVER
THE HEAD OF A PIN

## Colourful scales

A butterfly's wings are covered in thin dust-like scales arranged in over-lapping rows, like tiles on a roof. The scales are designed to colour the surface of the wing and produce intricate patterns.

THESE SCALES ARE
FROM THE BLUE UPPER
WING OF THE MORPHO
BUTTERFLY

THE POSITIONS OF THE
RIDGES MAKE BLUE THE
DOMINANT COLOUR

THE PARALLEL RIDGES
ARE FINE AND EVENLY
SPACED

A SCALE CAN ALSO
CONTAIN PIGMENT
WHICH CAN CREATE
ADDITIONAL
COLOURS

A 'Y'-SHAPED SUPPORT

THE BASE OF A SCALE ON THE
BUTTERFLY'S WING

UNDER A MICROSCOPE, THE
RIDGES ON A SINGLE SCALE
ARE VISIBLE

## Butterfly scales

Each butterfly scale is made up of parallel ridges, held up by supports. The ridges reflect each colour – metallic blues, greens, and purples in a different direction.

## Stick insects

Stick insects are aptly named. Keeping very still on a branch they are difficult to see. Their body, legs, and antennae are long and thin, resembling small sticks. When they move, they do so very slowly.

## Insect twig

Many moth caterpillars, including 'inch worms', are very thin and coloured like plants. Holding on to a twig with their rear sucker-like legs, they often extend out stiffly, pretending to be a short shoot.

## Not what it seems

Some caterpillars and pupae have a strange way of disguising themselves. They pretend to be bird droppings – enough to put any predator off.

# Feeding

INSECTS CAN eat almost anything! Their versatile mouth parts can cut, lick, and suck. Food is taken in through the mouth and enters the long alimentary canal or gut, which is divided into three parts: the fore-gut, mid-gut, and hind-gut. Both the fore-gut and the hind-gut are lined with a thin layer of cuticle. The fore-gut begins with the oesophagus. This leads to the thorax, where it widens to form the crop. Food is stored in the crop before being passed on to the gizzard where it is ground up. The gizzard is lined with thick cuticle and spines or ridges. The mid-gut is not lined with cuticle, and digested food can be absorbed here. The hind-gut is a coiled tube divided into three parts: the ileum, colon, and rectum.

FAECAL MATTER (WASTE) IS FORMED IN THE COLON

WASTE IS PASSED OUT THROUGH THE ANUS

THE RECTUM ABSORBS WATER AND IMPORTANT SALTS

THESE FINE TUBULES FILTER AND CLEAN THE BLOOD OF WASTE WHICH IS PASSED INTO THE COLON

THE ILEUM ABSORBS THE DIGESTED FOOD INTO THE BLOOD

THE AMERICAN COCKROACH CAN SURVIVE FOR THREE MONTHS WITHOUT FOOD BY LIVING OFF STORES IN ITS BODY

①

②

③

④

⑤

## Mouth parts

A housefly (1) moistens its food with saliva before licking it. The food and saliva are then sucked up. A mosquito's mouth (2) consists of a tube which contains a set of cutting tools. Females pierce the skin of their prey so blood can be sucked up. Males feed on plant juices.

Butterflies (3) have an elongated, coiled mouth part called a proboscis, which sucks up nectar. Bees (4) have licking and biting mouth parts. The mandibles can bite while the tongue can lap-up nectar. Bush crickets (5) are scavengers and hunters. They have powerful mouth parts for biting and cutting.

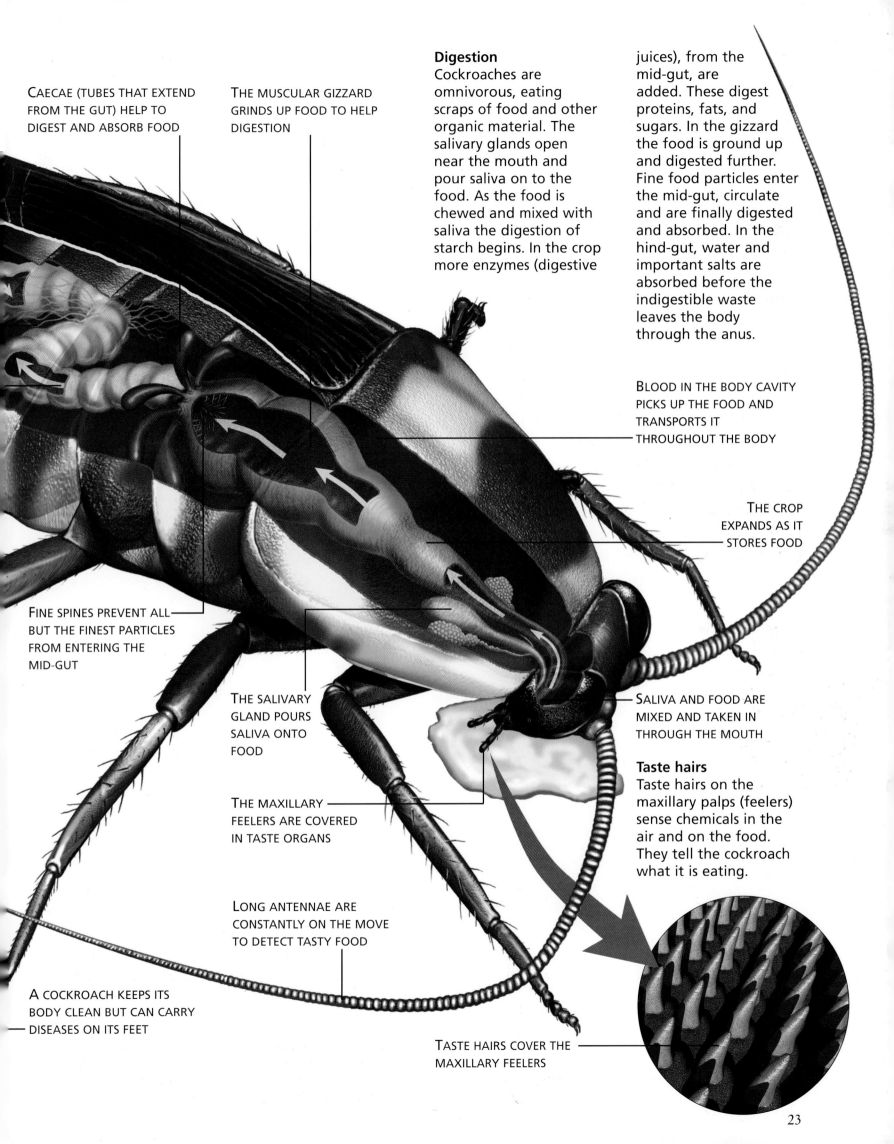

CAECAE (TUBES THAT EXTEND FROM THE GUT) HELP TO DIGEST AND ABSORB FOOD

THE MUSCULAR GIZZARD GRINDS UP FOOD TO HELP DIGESTION

## Digestion

Cockroaches are omnivorous, eating scraps of food and other organic material. The salivary glands open near the mouth and pour saliva on to the food. As the food is chewed and mixed with saliva the digestion of starch begins. In the crop more enzymes (digestive juices), from the mid-gut, are added. These digest proteins, fats, and sugars. In the gizzard the food is ground up and digested further. Fine food particles enter the mid-gut, circulate and are finally digested and absorbed. In the hind-gut, water and important salts are absorbed before the indigestible waste leaves the body through the anus.

BLOOD IN THE BODY CAVITY PICKS UP THE FOOD AND TRANSPORTS IT THROUGHOUT THE BODY

THE CROP EXPANDS AS IT STORES FOOD

FINE SPINES PREVENT ALL BUT THE FINEST PARTICLES FROM ENTERING THE MID-GUT

THE SALIVARY GLAND POURS SALIVA ONTO FOOD

SALIVA AND FOOD ARE MIXED AND TAKEN IN THROUGH THE MOUTH

## Taste hairs

Taste hairs on the maxillary palps (feelers) sense chemicals in the air and on the food. They tell the cockroach what it is eating.

THE MAXILLARY FEELERS ARE COVERED IN TASTE ORGANS

LONG ANTENNAE ARE CONSTANTLY ON THE MOVE TO DETECT TASTY FOOD

A COCKROACH KEEPS ITS BODY CLEAN BUT CAN CARRY DISEASES ON ITS FEET

TASTE HAIRS COVER THE MAXILLARY FEELERS

# Parasites

BLOOD FROM a living animal can make a tasty meal for some insects. Blood-sucking insects are called parasites and their food source is a live host. Living on another animal can be difficult. The host does not want them and will try to remove them. For example, to survive any attempts by the host to be pulled or shaken off, a flea (*right*), has stout bristles, hairs, and hooks to help it grip the host's hair. Strong claws also grip the host's skin. A flea's exoskeleton is very thick, tough, and slippery, making it hard for the host to squash or grip it. Using its powerful legs, it can jump away from danger and jump back onto its host. The flea's thin body enables it to squeeze between the host's hairs. Its special mouth parts are designed to penetrate the host's skin to reach the blood beneath and draw it up into the flea's large, expandable gut.

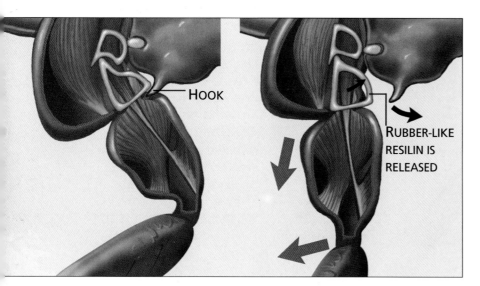

HOOK

RUBBER-LIKE RESILIN IS RELEASED

### Jumping legs
Powerful muscles pull the leg up against a hook on the flea's body distorting a piece of rubber-like cuticle called resilin. A sideways movement of the top of the leg pulls the hook off the catch, straightens the pad, releasing all the energy stored in the pad (like twanging a stretched elastic band). The leg is catapulted down, projecting the flea up to 40 centimetres into the air!

### Digestion
Ground-up blood from the crop is squirted into the mid-gut and mixed with enzymes. It then moves back up to the mid-gut wall where it is absorbed into the blood stream.

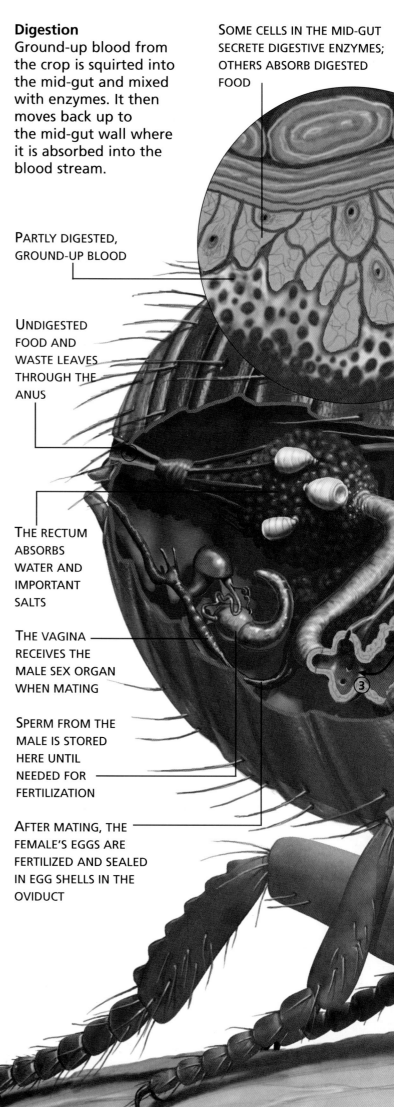

SOME CELLS IN THE MID-GUT SECRETE DIGESTIVE ENZYMES; OTHERS ABSORB DIGESTED FOOD

PARTLY DIGESTED, GROUND-UP BLOOD

UNDIGESTED FOOD AND WASTE LEAVES THROUGH THE ANUS

THE RECTUM ABSORBS WATER AND IMPORTANT SALTS

THE VAGINA RECEIVES THE MALE SEX ORGAN WHEN MATING

SPERM FROM THE MALE IS STORED HERE UNTIL NEEDED FOR FERTILIZATION

AFTER MATING, THE FEMALE'S EGGS ARE FERTILIZED AND SEALED IN EGG SHELLS IN THE OVIDUCT

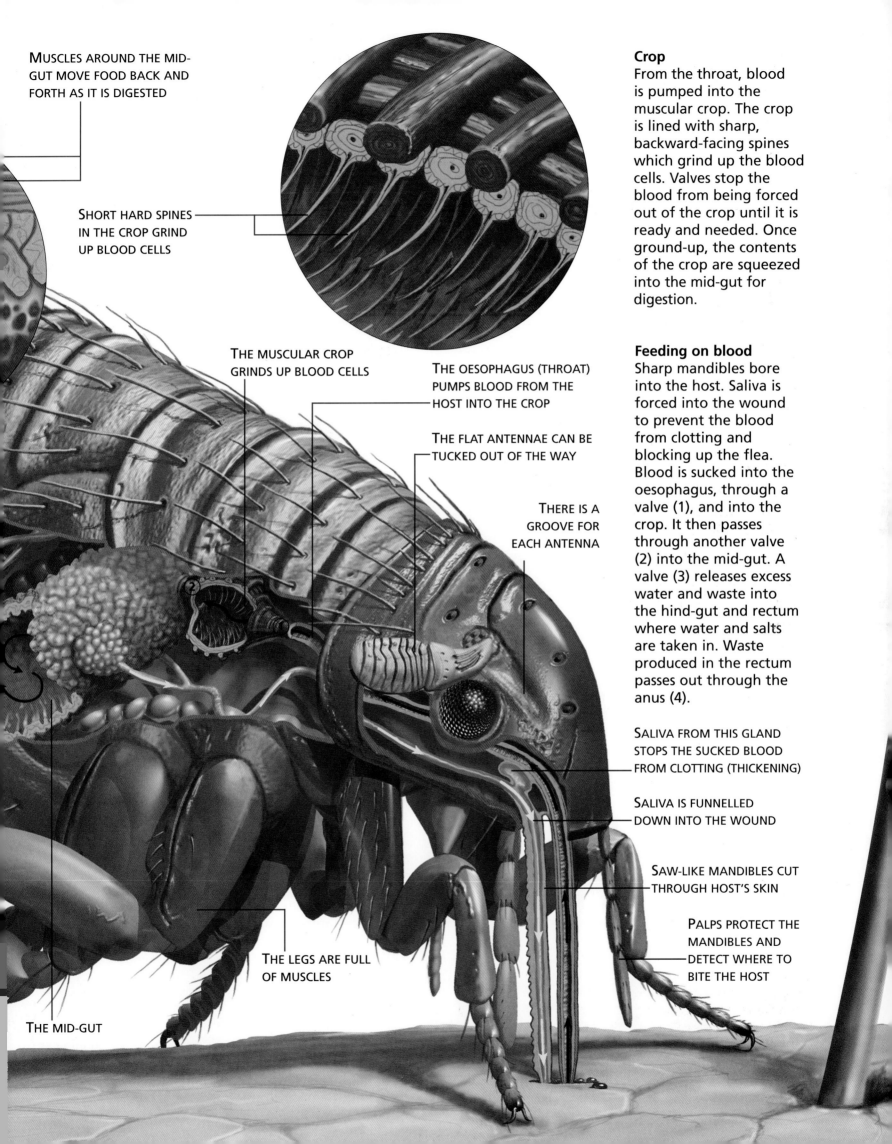

MUSCLES AROUND THE MID-GUT MOVE FOOD BACK AND FORTH AS IT IS DIGESTED

SHORT HARD SPINES IN THE CROP GRIND UP BLOOD CELLS

THE MUSCULAR CROP GRINDS UP BLOOD CELLS

THE OESOPHAGUS (THROAT) PUMPS BLOOD FROM THE HOST INTO THE CROP

THE FLAT ANTENNAE CAN BE TUCKED OUT OF THE WAY

THERE IS A GROOVE FOR EACH ANTENNA

THE LEGS ARE FULL OF MUSCLES

THE MID-GUT

## Crop

From the throat, blood is pumped into the muscular crop. The crop is lined with sharp, backward-facing spines which grind up the blood cells. Valves stop the blood from being forced out of the crop until it is ready and needed. Once ground-up, the contents of the crop are squeezed into the mid-gut for digestion.

## Feeding on blood

Sharp mandibles bore into the host. Saliva is forced into the wound to prevent the blood from clotting and blocking up the flea. Blood is sucked into the oesophagus, through a valve (1), and into the crop. It then passes through another valve (2) into the mid-gut. A valve (3) releases excess water and waste into the hind-gut and rectum where water and salts are taken in. Waste produced in the rectum passes out through the anus (4).

SALIVA FROM THIS GLAND STOPS THE SUCKED BLOOD FROM CLOTTING (THICKENING)

SALIVA IS FUNNELLED DOWN INTO THE WOUND

SAW-LIKE MANDIBLES CUT THROUGH HOST'S SKIN

PALPS PROTECT THE MANDIBLES AND DETECT WHERE TO BITE THE HOST

# Mating

AN INSECT'S main purpose in life is to reproduce. Some insects do not even feed, they just mate, lay eggs, and die. Like most other female animals, a female insect produces eggs from a pair of ovaries. The eggs travel down to her uterus where they are fertilized by sperm produced by the male. The sperm are made in a pair of organs, called the testes, inside the male. As with most insects, when longhorn beetles mate (*right*), the transfer of sperm from the male to the female is direct – they are injected into the female. This makes sure that the sperm are safe. Some male insects leave packets of sperm on the ground for the female to pick up. Shown right is a male longhorn beetle on the back of a female. He has climbed onto her and inserted his sex organ into her. Sperm pumps through this organ into the female. The sperm may be used straight away or stored until needed.

**Fighting for territory**
Rhinoceros beetles are so-named because the males are armed with 'horns'. They fight each other over the possession of a place where females they can mate with are likely to be. They try to turn each other over. The winner takes possession of the area and the looser leaves.

THE FEMALE LONGHORN BEETLE KEEPS A SHARP LOOK OUT FOR PREDATORS

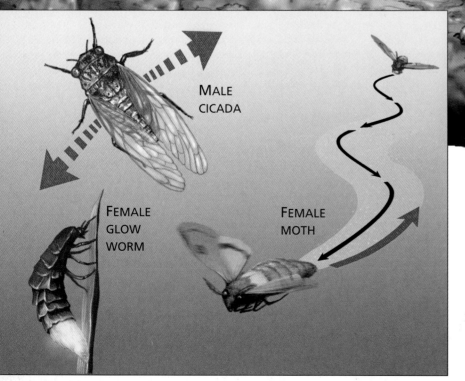

MALE CICADA

FEMALE GLOW WORM

FEMALE MOTH

**Ways of finding a mate**
Male cicadas use sound. They 'sing', bringing the males together and attracting females to them. Finding a mate through sight is important, too. Glow worms take this to the extreme. The females emit light at dusk to attract males. Many insects use smell. The female moth releases tiny amounts of chemicals called pheromones, which can be smelt by a male many miles away. He follows the scent to find her.

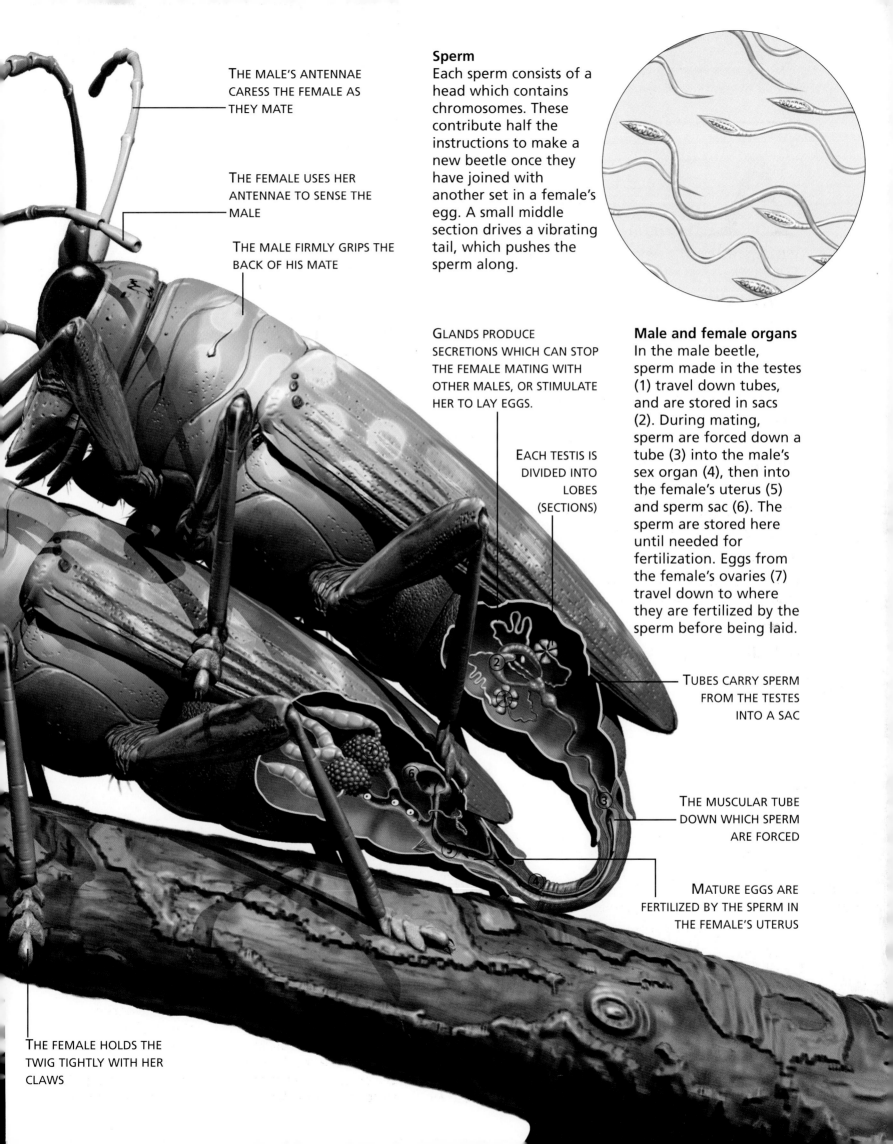

THE MALE'S ANTENNAE CARESS THE FEMALE AS THEY MATE

THE FEMALE USES HER ANTENNAE TO SENSE THE MALE

THE MALE FIRMLY GRIPS THE BACK OF HIS MATE

## Sperm

Each sperm consists of a head which contains chromosomes. These contribute half the instructions to make a new beetle once they have joined with another set in a female's egg. A small middle section drives a vibrating tail, which pushes the sperm along.

GLANDS PRODUCE SECRETIONS WHICH CAN STOP THE FEMALE MATING WITH OTHER MALES, OR STIMULATE HER TO LAY EGGS.

EACH TESTIS IS DIVIDED INTO LOBES (SECTIONS)

## Male and female organs

In the male beetle, sperm made in the testes (1) travel down tubes, and are stored in sacs (2). During mating, sperm are forced down a tube (3) into the male's sex organ (4), then into the female's uterus (5) and sperm sac (6). The sperm are stored here until needed for fertilization. Eggs from the female's ovaries (7) travel down to where they are fertilized by the sperm before being laid.

TUBES CARRY SPERM FROM THE TESTES INTO A SAC

THE MUSCULAR TUBE DOWN WHICH SPERM ARE FORCED

MATURE EGGS ARE FERTILIZED BY THE SPERM IN THE FEMALE'S UTERUS

THE FEMALE HOLDS THE TWIG TIGHTLY WITH HER CLAWS

# New Life

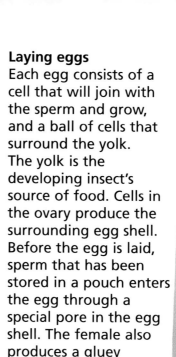

ADULT insects are mainly concerned with producing their young and making sure they are safe and have plenty of food to eat. After being fertilized by a male the female butterfly finds a place to lay her eggs – a suitable plant that will provide her offspring with food and as much protection from predators as possible. She then lays an egg or several eggs. Each egg is an amazing structure. It is not only filled with a rich yolk for the developing embryo to eat, but it is also tough and waterproof, to seal in moisture while the egg is exposed to the dry air. After being laid it may take from several days to several weeks, depending on the surrounding temperature, for the embryo in the egg to develop and hatch.

**Laying eggs**
Each egg consists of a cell that will join with the sperm and grow, and a ball of cells that surround the yolk. The yolk is the developing insect's source of food. Cells in the ovary produce the surrounding egg shell. Before the egg is laid, sperm that has been stored in a pouch enters the egg through a special pore in the egg shell. The female also produces a gluey substance to stick the egg down.

EACH OVARY PRODUCES OOCYTES RICH IN YOLK

THE OOCYTES GROW AND DEVELOP INTO A BALL OF CELLS

THE EGGS ARE FERTILIZED BY STORED SPERM FROM THE MALE

A NETWORK OF FINE PORES LETS THE EGG BREATHE AND KEEPS WATER IN

RIGID SUPPORTS ARE CONNECTED TO COLUMNS BENEATH

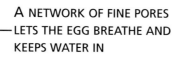

SPECIAL GLANDS HELP THE EGG-LAYING PROCESS

THE BREATHING AREA OF THE EGG IS PROTECTED BY A HOLLOW

THE LAID EGGS ARE STUCK FIRMLY TO A PLANT

WHEN THE EGGS HATCH THE PLANT WILL BE A FOOD SOURCE FOR THE YOUNG CATERPILLARS

**Egg shell structure**
Through a microscope we can see complicated patterns of pores on the surface of the egg shell. These lead into cavities beneath which let the egg breathe without losing precious water. Many insect eggs allow the developing embryo to breathe in both wet and dry conditions, in case the egg is covered by a rain drop.

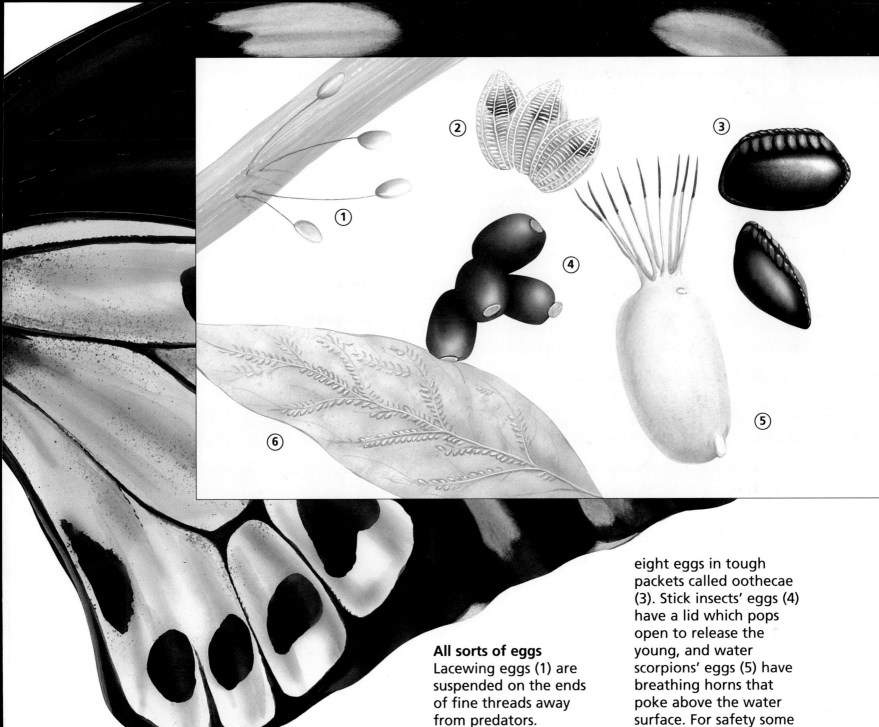

## All sorts of eggs

Lacewing eggs (1) are suspended on the ends of fine threads away from predators. Butterflies glue their tiny flask-shaped eggs (2) to plants. Cockroaches lay eight eggs in tough packets called oothecae (3). Stick insects' eggs (4) have a lid which pops open to release the young, and water scorpions' eggs (5) have breathing horns that poke above the water surface. For safety some sawflies lay their eggs (6) inside leaves close to the veins.

---

BEFORE FERTILIZATION THE EGG IS CALLED AN OOCYTE

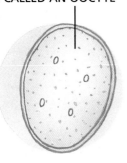

A BALL OF CELLS SURROUND THE YOLK

ONCE FERTILIZED, THE EGG IS CALLED A ZYGOTE

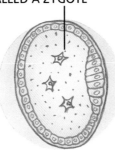

THE DEVELOPING EMBRYO SHOWS AN INSECT SHAPE

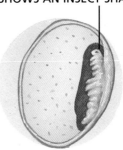

## Embryo development

Before fertilization the egg cell divides to form a sphere of cells called an oocyte, with some scattered cells drifting in the yolk. The cells continue to divide. The egg shell is produced by the outer cells. One cell is fertilized by the sperm from the male and the egg is laid. The fertilized cell, called a zygote, divides and forms the embryo, which will develop into the young insect. At this stage the beginnings of the mouth parts, antennae, and legs can just be seen. Once developed the egg hatches and a pupae will crawl out.

# Changing Shape

**M**ANY INSECTS hatch from eggs as nymphs, which moult (shed their outer skin) and gradually change into a different, adult form. But others, such as butterflies, are 'born' twice – once from their egg and a second time from their pupa. A butterfly emerges first in caterpillar form. Its soft cuticle (outer skin) allows its body to expand as it eats and grows. When the cuticle becomes too tight it is shed and the caterpillar continues to get larger. After a few weeks, the caterpillar changes into a chrysalis, or pupa. It spends this final stage in a pupa or case. About a month later the adult butterfly hatches, ready to find a mate and produce more butterflies.

## 7) New butterfly
Immediately after breaking out, the new butterfly has to stretch and expand its wings by pumping blood down the wing veins. The expanded wings then dry out, and the butterfly uses them to carry it off into the air.

## 6) Emergence
About a month after the chrysalis was formed, and the process of change is complete, the adult butterfly emerges from its chrysalis. Puffing itself up with air causes the case to split open, allowing the butterfly to crawl free.

POWERFUL WINGS HELP THE BUTTERFLY TO FIND FOOD AND A MATE, AND TO ESCAPE FROM PREDATORS

AN ADULT BUTTERFLY EMERGES FROM ITS CHRYSALIS ABOUT TWO MONTHS AFTER AN EGG WAS LAID

AIR CAN PASS THROUGH SPECIAL HOLES AT THE TOP

## 1) Eggs
The female butterfly lays clusters of eggs on a plant, which will provide food for the caterpillars after they hatch. The eggs keep the developing caterpillars safe from drying out and enable them to breathe.

## 2) Hatching
All the eggs hatch at the same time. The young caterpillar bites its way out at the top. It crawls out and eats the egg shell before it starts eating the plant.

A CATERPILLAR SHEDS ITS SKIN (MOULTS) SEVERAL TIMES AS IT GROWS BIGGER

A LARGER, SOFT NEW SKIN ENABLES FURTHER GROWTH

THE EGGS HATCH EIGHT DAYS AFTER BEING LAID

IT SHEDS ITS OLD SKIN

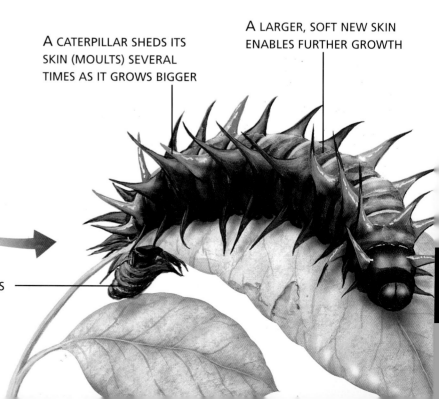

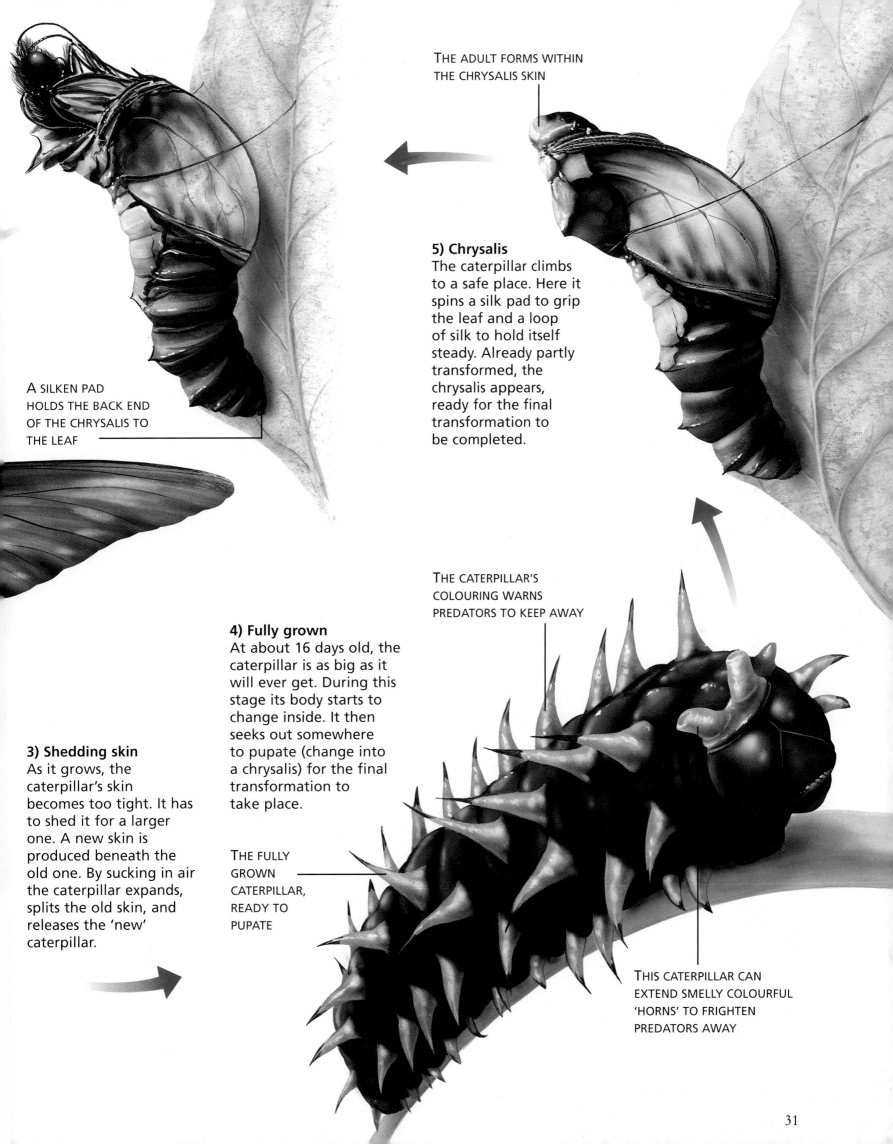

THE ADULT FORMS WITHIN THE CHRYSALIS SKIN

A SILKEN PAD HOLDS THE BACK END OF THE CHRYSALIS TO THE LEAF

## 5) Chrysalis

The caterpillar climbs to a safe place. Here it spins a silk pad to grip the leaf and a loop of silk to hold itself steady. Already partly transformed, the chrysalis appears, ready for the final transformation to be completed.

THE CATERPILLAR'S COLOURING WARNS PREDATORS TO KEEP AWAY

## 4) Fully grown

At about 16 days old, the caterpillar is as big as it will ever get. During this stage its body starts to change inside. It then seeks out somewhere to pupate (change into a chrysalis) for the final transformation to take place.

## 3) Shedding skin

As it grows, the caterpillar's skin becomes too tight. It has to shed it for a larger one. A new skin is produced beneath the old one. By sucking in air the caterpillar expands, splits the old skin, and releases the 'new' caterpillar.

THE FULLY GROWN CATERPILLAR, READY TO PUPATE

THIS CATERPILLAR CAN EXTEND SMELLY COLOURFUL 'HORNS' TO FRIGHTEN PREDATORS AWAY

# Ants' Nest

ANTS LIVE together in complex societies. There are over 5,000 different kinds of ant community. Each nest is headed by a queen who is cared for by her daughters, the female workers. Some ants have different types of workers, called castes, which do different tasks. Ants build their nests in all kinds of places. Here, the nest is on the ground and extends under it. Workers burrow in the soil and pile up the material from below on the surface above. This has been made into a mound full of tunnels and chambers. In the maze of tunnels and chambers the queen ant lives, the eggs and larvae are cared for, and food is stored. At certain times, winged queens and males are produced. These leave the nest to mate.

## Egg-laying queen

The queen is much larger than her workers. She is the only ant in the nest that lays eggs. As the eggs are laid they are looked after by attendant workers. On hatching, the young larvae are moved to other chambers where they become pupae (chrysalises). Ants will emerge from the pupae.

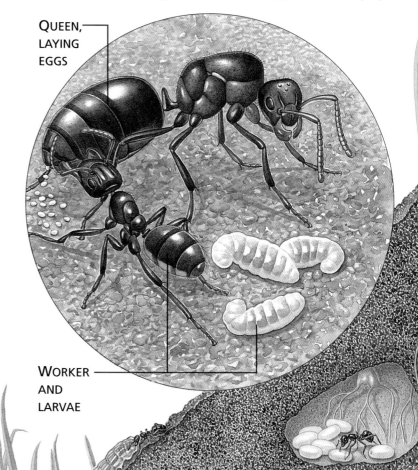

QUEEN, LAYING EGGS

WORKER AND LARVAE

A WORKER ANT HERDING APHIDS FOR THEIR HONEYDEW

A CATERPILLAR IS DRAGGED BACK TO THE NEST FOR FOOD

②

## Herding aphids

To feed, tiny insects called aphids suck plant sap. This sap contains a lot of water and sugar, far more than the aphids need, so they secrete the excess from the ends of their bodies. Ants have a very sweet tooth and collect this sugary liquid called honeydew. To make the aphids produce more, the ants stimulate them by stroking their backs, milking them like cows. The ants also look after the aphids, guarding them from predators.

SECRETIONS FROM THE WORKERS STOP THE EGGS AND LARVAE GOING MOULDY

QUEEN CHAMBER WITH THE EGG-LAYING QUEEN AND WORKERS TENDING THE EGGS AND LARVAE

THE SUN'S RAYS WARM THE NEST

HONEY POT ANTS

LEAF-CUTTER ANTS

HARVESTER ANTS

GRASSES ARE SLOWLY BURIED BY SOIL AS THE NEST GROWS

WINGED QUEENS (LARGE) AND WINGED MALES (SMALL) EMERGE FROM THE NEST TO MATE

## Ant variety

Ants eat plants, honey-dew, nectar, fungi and other insects. Some species of ant collect honeydew which they feed to special workers whose abdomens swell like grapes making them into living honey-pots! Leaf-cutter ants eat fungus that grows on the plant pieces they collect. Harvester ants collect seeds, dry them in the sun, then store them for eating later.

SPECIAL TUNNELS ARE DUG TO RELEASE QUEENS AND MALES.

③

A WORKER SETS OFF ON A TRIP TO FORAGE FOR FOOD

A WORKER TAKES A LARVA TO ANOTHER CHAMBER

THE SOIL IS CHEWED INTO FINE DUST AS THE ANTS DIG OUT THE NEST'S CHAMBERS AND TUNNELS

WORKERS LOOK AFTER PUPAE WHICH WILL SOON HATCH

## Ants' home life

An ant mound absorbs the sun's heat, keeping the nest warm. In the royal chamber (1) the queen lays her eggs which are taken to other chambers (2) to be cared for. The larvae are moved to nursery chambers (3) where they will change into pupae. Other chambers are food stores. Tunnels connect the chambers and let workers get to the outside to forage.

# Bees' Nest

HONEYBEE nests are busy places. In each nest a bustling community of up to 60,000 insects live together. Nearly all the bees are females, called workers, which hatch from fertilized eggs laid by the queen who is in charge of the colony. A few males that hatch from unfertilized eggs appear during the summer and autumn. They do not work as their only job is to mate with new queens. All the worker bees live together, building and looking after their home, collecting food and water, feeding the young and caring for the queen. They secrete wax to make their nest. Sheets of strong hexagonal cells hang down and hold the eggs, larvae, nectar (which becomes honey) and pollen. Being able to store food allows honeybees to live through times when food is scarce, such as the winter.

A DRONE (MALE BEE) HAS LARGE EYES FOR FINDING YOUNG QUEENS TO MATE WITH

AN INNER CRESCENT OF CELLS IS FILLED WITH POLLEN, A PROTEIN-RICH FOOD

THE OUTER CELLS ARE FILLED WITH NECTAR WHICH IS TURNED INTO HONEY BY THE BEES; THE CELL IS THEN SEALED

A WORKER BEE, CALLED A FORAGER, BRINGS BACK POLLEN TO FEED THE YOUNG

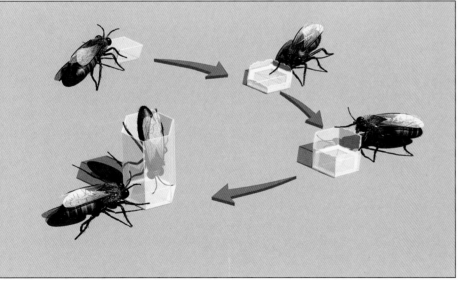

**Building cells**
A worker bee produces scales of wax from glands under its abdomen. These are spread onto a surface using its jaws. More wax is added and shaped into a hexagonal cell.

Cells are produced together, forming a sheet of honeycomb with cells on both sides, each angled slightly upwards. Combs hang side by side, just close enough to allow two bees to pass each other.

A FORAGER SETS OFF IN SEARCH OF POLLEN, NECTAR, WATER, OR ANY OTHER ITEM THE COLONY MAY NEED

BEES COMMUNICATE WITH EACH OTHER BY PASSING FOOD AND CHEMICALS FROM THE QUEEN

A WORKER BEE MAY TRAVEL 2.5 KILOMETRES TO FIND NECTAR

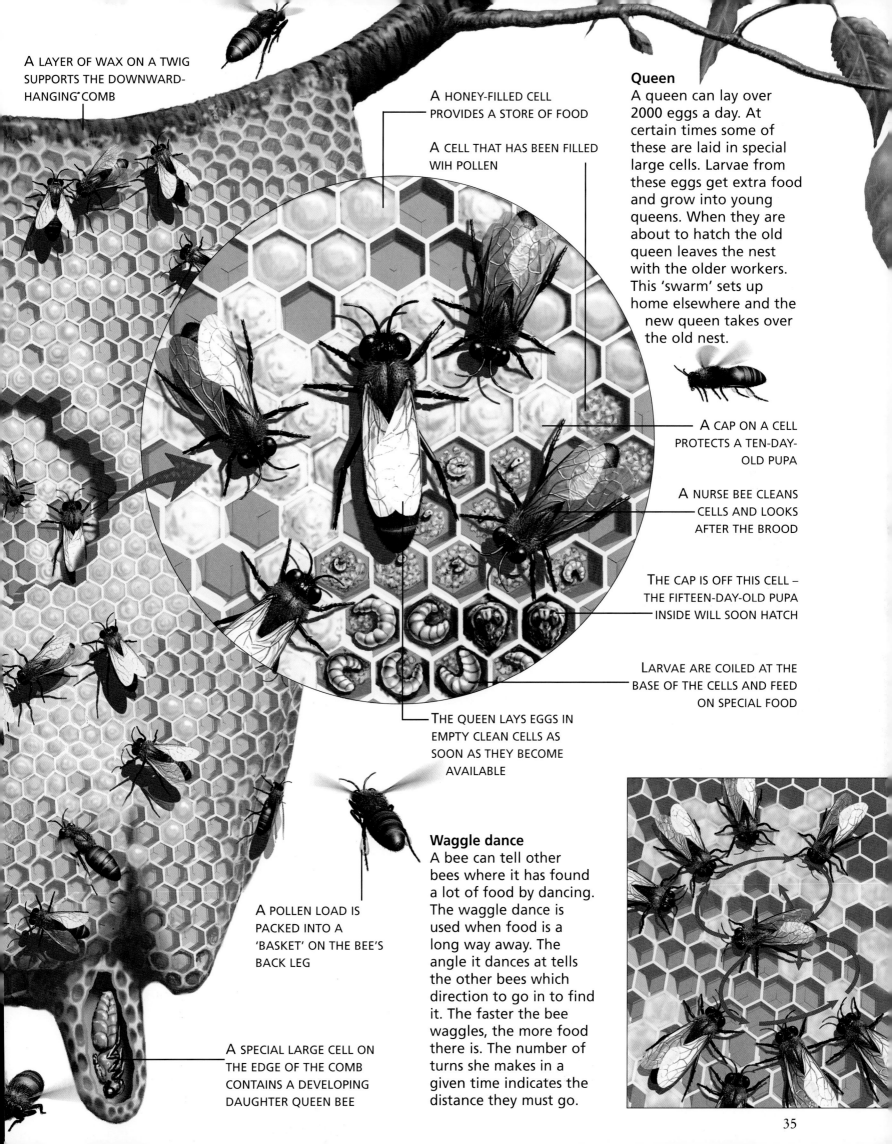

A LAYER OF WAX ON A TWIG SUPPORTS THE DOWNWARD-HANGING COMB

A HONEY-FILLED CELL PROVIDES A STORE OF FOOD

A CELL THAT HAS BEEN FILLED WIH POLLEN

## Queen
A queen can lay over 2000 eggs a day. At certain times some of these are laid in special large cells. Larvae from these eggs get extra food and grow into young queens. When they are about to hatch the old queen leaves the nest with the older workers. This 'swarm' sets up home elsewhere and the new queen takes over the old nest.

A CAP ON A CELL PROTECTS A TEN-DAY-OLD PUPA

A NURSE BEE CLEANS CELLS AND LOOKS AFTER THE BROOD

THE CAP IS OFF THIS CELL – THE FIFTEEN-DAY-OLD PUPA INSIDE WILL SOON HATCH

LARVAE ARE COILED AT THE BASE OF THE CELLS AND FEED ON SPECIAL FOOD

THE QUEEN LAYS EGGS IN EMPTY CLEAN CELLS AS SOON AS THEY BECOME AVAILABLE

A POLLEN LOAD IS PACKED INTO A 'BASKET' ON THE BEE'S BACK LEG

A SPECIAL LARGE CELL ON THE EDGE OF THE COMB CONTAINS A DEVELOPING DAUGHTER QUEEN BEE

## Waggle dance
A bee can tell other bees where it has found a lot of food by dancing. The waggle dance is used when food is a long way away. The angle it dances at tells the other bees which direction to go in to find it. The faster the bee waggles, the more food there is. The number of turns she makes in a given time indicates the distance they must go.

# Rainforest Life

TROPICAL heat and moisture are ideal for the growth of rainforests. Here, insects are the most numerous and varied form of animal life. Nearly 200 species of butterfly can be found in one hectare of South East Asian rainforest alone. However, we do not know how many rainforest insects there are in total – there may still be millions to discover. Insects can be difficult to see as many fly high in the tree-tops, and many are so well camouflaged that they look just like a flower, thorn or leaf. Others live hidden inside rotting wood, living plants, or leaves. Insects are a very important part of forest life – they pollinate plants and help to recycle waste matter into reusable nutrients.

**Grasshoppers**
Powerful back legs allow grasshoppers to jump out of the way of danger. These green nymphs are well camouflaged and difficult to see in the forest.

GRASSHOPPER NYMPHS (YOUNG)

**Mantis**
This is not a pretty flower, but a dangerous predator! Disguised to match the flower upon which it sits, this mantis waits patiently for an insect to visit the flower – then it will pounce.

MANTIS

THESE TREE HOPPERS CAN SUCK PLANT SAP IN SAFETY – THEY ARE DISGUISED AS THORNS, HENCE THEIR OTHER NAME: THORNBUGS

POISONOUS SPINES ON CATERPILLARS STOP PREDATORS FROM THINKING THEY ARE AN EASY MEAL

**Leaf-cutter ants**
Strong leaf-cutter ants cut pieces of leaves and carry them to their nest. They eat the fungus that begins to grow on the leaf pieces.

A LEAF-CUTTER ANT CARRYING A PIECE OF LEAF BACK TO ITS NEST

NOT A DEAD LEAF BUT A LEAF INSECT

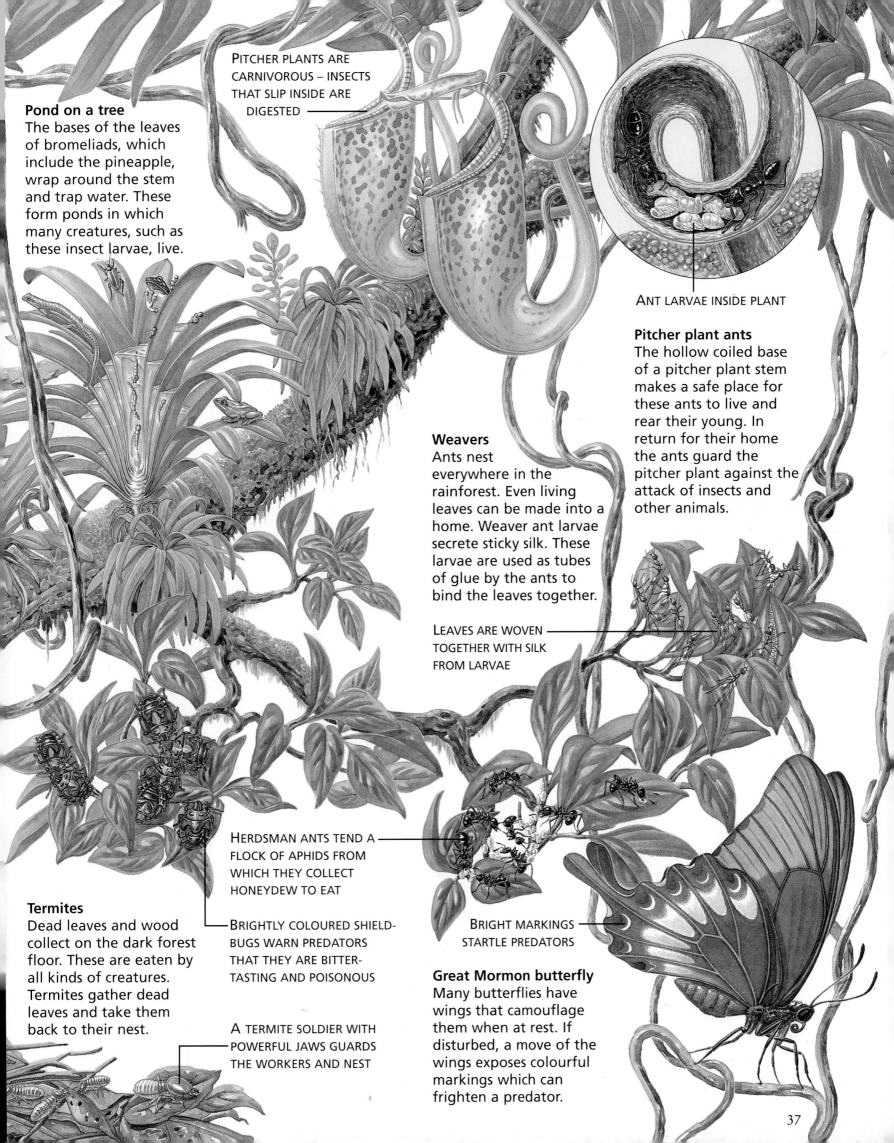

**Pond on a tree**
The bases of the leaves of bromeliads, which include the pineapple, wrap around the stem and trap water. These form ponds in which many creatures, such as these insect larvae, live.

PITCHER PLANTS ARE CARNIVOROUS – INSECTS THAT SLIP INSIDE ARE DIGESTED

ANT LARVAE INSIDE PLANT

**Pitcher plant ants**
The hollow coiled base of a pitcher plant stem makes a safe place for these ants to live and rear their young. In return for their home the ants guard the pitcher plant against the attack of insects and other animals.

**Weavers**
Ants nest everywhere in the rainforest. Even living leaves can be made into a home. Weaver ant larvae secrete sticky silk. These larvae are used as tubes of glue by the ants to bind the leaves together.

LEAVES ARE WOVEN TOGETHER WITH SILK FROM LARVAE

HERDSMAN ANTS TEND A FLOCK OF APHIDS FROM WHICH THEY COLLECT HONEYDEW TO EAT

**Termites**
Dead leaves and wood collect on the dark forest floor. These are eaten by all kinds of creatures. Termites gather dead leaves and take them back to their nest.

BRIGHTLY COLOURED SHIELD-BUGS WARN PREDATORS THAT THEY ARE BITTER-TASTING AND POISONOUS

A TERMITE SOLDIER WITH POWERFUL JAWS GUARDS THE WORKERS AND NEST

BRIGHT MARKINGS STARTLE PREDATORS

**Great Mormon butterfly**
Many butterflies have wings that camouflage them when at rest. If disturbed, a move of the wings exposes colourful markings which can frighten a predator.

# Insects in Water

MANY TYPES of insect live in freshwater at some time in their lives. Several, including flies such as the dragonfly as well as true flies, only spend the earliest part of their lives there – as nymphs (young which resemble the adult insect) or larvae (a worm-like form that does not resemble the adult until later on). Other freshwater insects, like beetles and bugs, live in water both during their early and adult stages. The adults also live on land, travelling through the air to new habitats. Because water can dissolve large amounts of oxygen, many insects are able to breathe in it. Most nymphs use gills to breathe, but other insects breathe at the water's surface. A few take a packet of air down with them when they dive, returning to the surface to get more when the oxygen runs out. Insects use their legs and even their wings to swim about.

**A mayfly's life**
Mayfly nymphs feed on dead vegetation and live in tubes in mud or crawl amongst aquatic plants. As adults, they have just a day to live. During that time they do not eat but only mate and lay eggs.

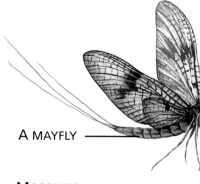

A MAYFLY

MOSQUITO LARVAE AND PUPAE BREATHE THROUGH THE SURFACE FILM OF THE WATER

WHIRLIGIG BEETLES SPIN AROUND ON THE SURFACE LOOKING FOR FOOD

AIR IS TRAPPED UNDER THE GREAT DIVING BEETLE'S WING COVERS

ITS LEGS PUSH AGAINST THE WATER, FORCING IT FORWARD

IT HAS BROAD OAR-LIKE BACK LEGS FOR SWIMMING

**Great diving beetle**
During adulthood and as larvae, these beetles are fast aggressive predators. Adults are sleek and smooth, and have broad oar-like back legs, fringed with bristles for rapid swimming. Their front legs are designed to grasp their prey. When they are under water, they breathe using air trapped in hairs beneath their wing covers.

THE DIVING BEETLE'S STRONG FRONT LEGS CAN GRASP PREY

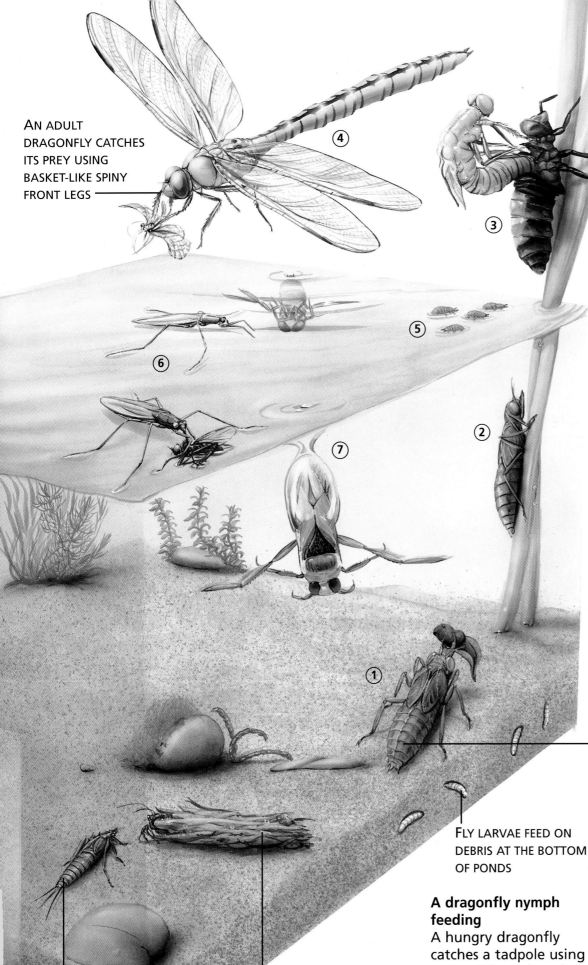

AN ADULT
DRAGONFLY CATCHES
ITS PREY USING
BASKET-LIKE SPINY
FRONT LEGS

**Life cycle of a dragonfly**
The dragonfly lays its eggs under water, in or on water plants. The eggs hatch as predatory nymphs (1). As each nymph grows, it moults and gradually changes. Eventually it crawls out of the water (2) and emerges as an adult dragonfly with tiny wings (3), which it inflates and dries before flying off in search of food or a mate (4).

**Life on the surface**
The surface film is home to several insect hunters and scavengers. Tiny wingless springtails called Podura (5) scavenge for food. They usually crawl but can also jump if disturbed. Aptly named pond skaters (6) are fast hunters but also take trapped and drowned prey. Water boatmen (7) hang from the surface of the water waiting for prey. With powerful legs it chases its victim, killing it with its stabbing mouth parts.

A DRAGONFLY NYMPH
CATCHES A TADPOLE USING
ITS 'MASK'

FLY LARVAE FEED ON
DEBRIS AT THE BOTTOM
OF PONDS

**A dragonfly nymph feeding**
A hungry dragonfly catches a tadpole using its special 'mask' mouth part. The 'mask' remains folded under the head until the nymph shoots it forward and catches the prey using the strong jaws at its tip.

THE CADDIS LARVA MAKES A
HOME OF STONES OR PLANT
REMAINS

A MAYFLY NYMPH SCURRIES
ALONG THE POND FLOOR
LOOKING FOR FOOD

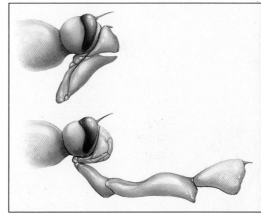

# Woodland Life

TREES MAKE perfect homes for many insects, providing plenty of food and places to shelter. One tree in particular, the oak, supports a huge variety of insect life, including over 210 species of moths and butterflies. Insects make use of all the tree – from the leaves, shoots, and flowers in the canopy to the roots underground. They chew the leaves from the outside and inside, burrow under the bark and into the wood, and live inside the tree's fruits, the acorns. As well as eating the tree they also use it as a refuge, hiding in the crevices of the bark. Other insects are parasites that live on other insects that feed on the plant. Still others are predators, searching and hunting for prey. Throughout the year different insects can be found on different parts of every tree in a woodland.

## Marble gall
Gall wasps have two types of larvae. Those of one species produce marble galls on one type of oak and bud-galls on another.

## Purple hairstreak
This butterfly only lives on oak. Its caterpillars feed at night on young leaves. When full grown they pupate in the soil. If taken into an ants' nest they are better protected from predators.

## Oak bark beetle
Just below the bark a female beetle makes a tunnel where she lays her eggs. The grubs that hatch make long vertical tunnels as they feed.

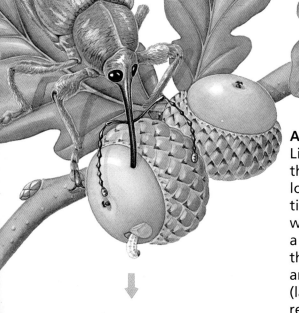

## Acorn weevil
Like all nut weevils the acorn weevil has a long thin snout. At its tip are the mandibles, which it uses to pierce a hole and bore into the acorn. Here it lays an egg, and the grub (larva) feeds in its ready-made larder. When the acorn falls, the grub comes out and develops into a pupa in the soil.

## Lacewing
Delicate lacewings are active in the evening. Both adults and larvae hunt aphids. The larvae camouflage themselves by sticking pieces of debris to their back, including the dried husks of their prey.

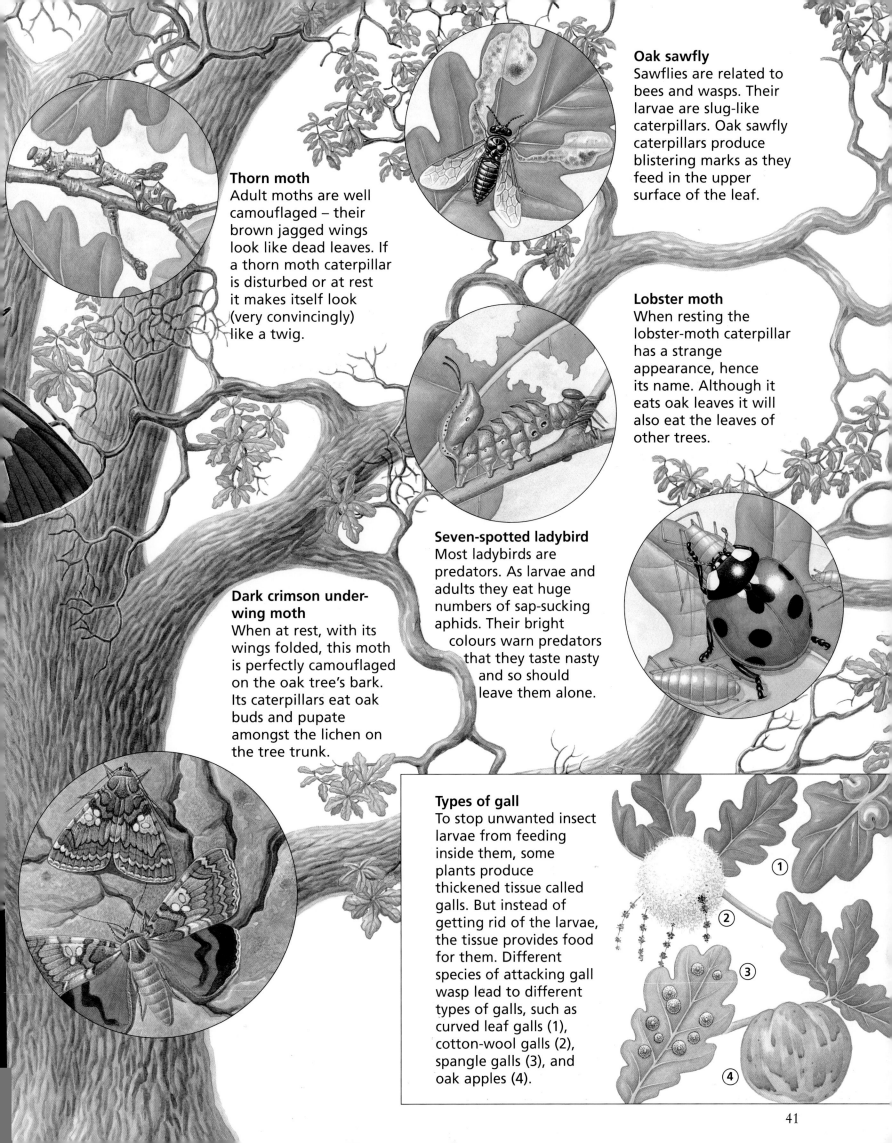

**Thorn moth**
Adult moths are well camouflaged – their brown jagged wings look like dead leaves. If a thorn moth caterpillar is disturbed or at rest it makes itself look (very convincingly) like a twig.

**Oak sawfly**
Sawflies are related to bees and wasps. Their larvae are slug-like caterpillars. Oak sawfly caterpillars produce blistering marks as they feed in the upper surface of the leaf.

**Lobster moth**
When resting the lobster-moth caterpillar has a strange appearance, hence its name. Although it eats oak leaves it will also eat the leaves of other trees.

**Seven-spotted ladybird**
Most ladybirds are predators. As larvae and adults they eat huge numbers of sap-sucking aphids. Their bright colours warn predators that they taste nasty and so should leave them alone.

**Dark crimson under-wing moth**
When at rest, with its wings folded, this moth is perfectly camouflaged on the oak tree's bark. Its caterpillars eat oak buds and pupate amongst the lichen on the tree trunk.

**Types of gall**
To stop unwanted insect larvae from feeding inside them, some plants produce thickened tissue called galls. But instead of getting rid of the larvae, the tissue provides food for them. Different species of attacking gall wasp lead to different types of galls, such as curved leaf galls (1), cotton-wool galls (2), spangle galls (3), and oak apples (4).

# Desert Insects

**D**ESERTS ARE mainly hot and dry, having little rainfall, so the environment is a difficult one for animals to survive in. Those that do are specially adapted to the harsh conditions. Many hide away during the extreme heat of the day, either under rocks, or buried in the sand or deep in burrows. Only at night and early morning when it is cool do they emerge to feed. Those insects that do come out during the day move from place to place quickly, keeping in the shade. Their feet are often specially adapted so that they are able to touch the hot sand when necessary, and they have a thick cuticle to reduce the loss of moisture. Some gather moisture to drink in the early morning mist, while others rely on the moisture in their food to sustain them. Even if they do lose water they can withstand a great deal of dehydration (water loss).

### Hunting wasp
A hunting wasp lives a solitary life. A female (1) digs a burrow and then hunts for insects. Using her sting she paralyses her prey and takes it back to the burrow. Here she lays an egg on it. The larva that hatches feeds on the living victim.

### Harvester ants
Harvester ants (2) nest underground, away from the sun's killing heat. Foragers gather seeds for food which they first dry in the sun before storing them in special chambers inside their nest. They eat the seeds as needed. They also eat insects such as caterpillars.

### Dune cricket
The dune cricket (3) uses its flower-shaped feet to dig in the sand to escape the heat of the sun and predators. When the temperature falls, the cricket emerges to feed on the sparse vegetation.

### Tiger beetle
Like a tiger in the jungle, a tiger beetle (4) hunts its prey. These agile and fast predators have powerful jaws to kill even quite large insects.

### Head-stander
Water droplets from early morning mist condense on this darkling beetle (5). It stands on tip-toe so the droplets run together and down to its mouth.

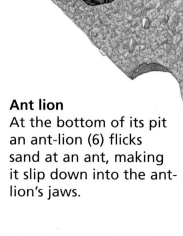

DEEP UNDER-GROUND, THE NEST CHAMBERS ARE COOL———

### Ant lion
At the bottom of its pit an ant-lion (6) flicks sand at an ant, making it slip down into the ant-lion's jaws.

42

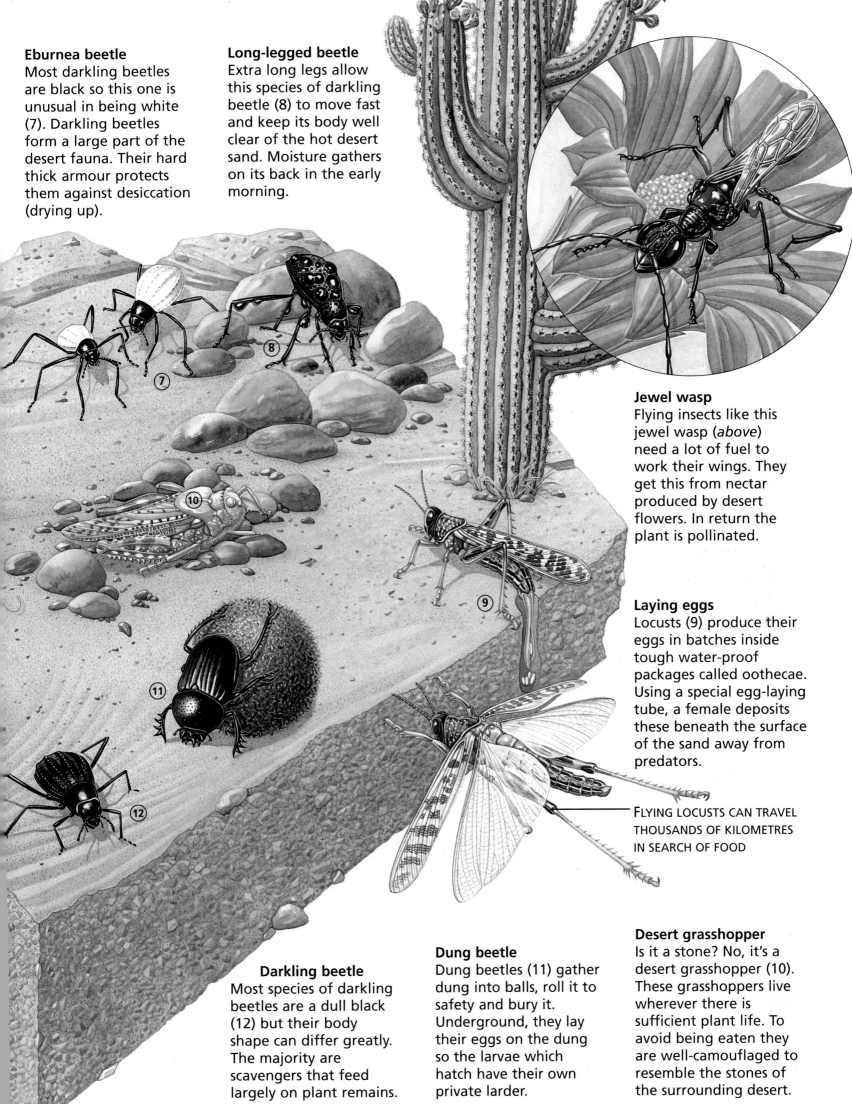

**Eburnea beetle**
Most darkling beetles are black so this one is unusual in being white (7). Darkling beetles form a large part of the desert fauna. Their hard thick armour protects them against desiccation (drying up).

**Long-legged beetle**
Extra long legs allow this species of darkling beetle (8) to move fast and keep its body well clear of the hot desert sand. Moisture gathers on its back in the early morning.

**Jewel wasp**
Flying insects like this jewel wasp (*above*) need a lot of fuel to work their wings. They get this from nectar produced by desert flowers. In return the plant is pollinated.

**Laying eggs**
Locusts (9) produce their eggs in batches inside tough water-proof packages called oothecae. Using a special egg-laying tube, a female deposits these beneath the surface of the sand away from predators.

FLYING LOCUSTS CAN TRAVEL THOUSANDS OF KILOMETRES IN SEARCH OF FOOD

**Darkling beetle**
Most species of darkling beetles are a dull black (12) but their body shape can differ greatly. The majority are scavengers that feed largely on plant remains.

**Dung beetle**
Dung beetles (11) gather dung into balls, roll it to safety and bury it. Underground, they lay their eggs on the dung so the larvae which hatch have their own private larder.

**Desert grasshopper**
Is it a stone? No, it's a desert grasshopper (10). These grasshoppers live wherever there is sufficient plant life. To avoid being eaten they are well-camouflaged to resemble the stones of the surrounding desert.

43

# Microscopic Life

HIDDEN AWAY in their secret worlds are thousands of microscopic insects. Insects are the most successful group of living animals on Earth partly because many of them make use of the tiniest of spaces – including the gaps between grains of cereal, the crevices of tree bark, and the fur of mammals. Within almost every group of insects there is a type that is microscopic. Despite their small size they are still made to the same body plan as their larger cousins. Breathing is easier for tiny insects, as the oxygen breathed in and the carbon dioxide breathed out only have to travel very short distances. But being small can be a problem. For example, flying in the air for them would be like swimming in treacle for humans, so their wings are specially designed to make it easier.

### Head louse

Head lice are a type of sucking lice that live in human hair. More than a thousand can live on one head, but the normal number is about a dozen. For camouflage they match the colour of the hair in which they live. Anyone can be a host to lice, catching them from other people and clothing. When feeding, the louse grabs a hair and stands on its head, gripping the scalp with a ring of hooks before inserting a long mouth-part into the skin to suck blood. They feed twice a day, causing irritation and sometimes disease.

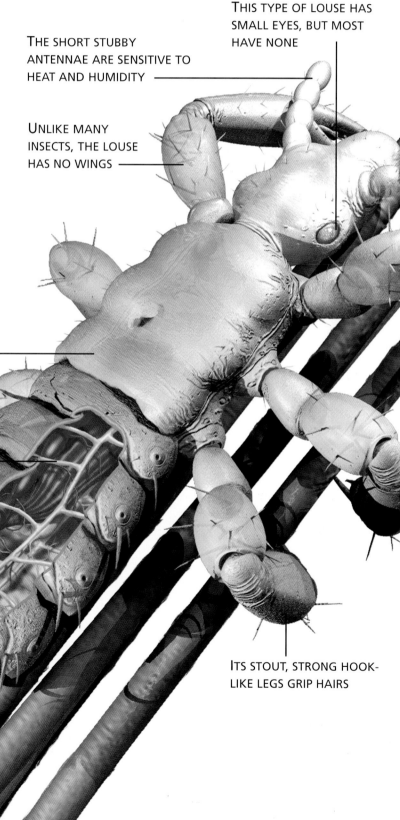

THIS TYPE OF LOUSE HAS SMALL EYES, BUT MOST HAVE NONE

THE SHORT STUBBY ANTENNAE ARE SENSITIVE TO HEAT AND HUMIDITY

UNLIKE MANY INSECTS, THE LOUSE HAS NO WINGS

ITS FLATTENED AND TOUGH BODY MAKES THE LOUSE HARD TO KILL AND REMOVE

BREATHING TUBES CALLED TRACHEA TAKE OXYGEN TO AND CARBON DIOXIDE AWAY FROM THE TISSUES

THE LOUSE'S HEART PUMPS BLOOD AROUND ITS BODY

THE LOUSE IS DARK WHEN ITS INTESTINES ARE FULL OF DIGESTED BLOOD

THE NERVOUS SYSTEM

SPINES

ITS STOUT, STRONG HOOK-LIKE LEGS GRIP HAIRS

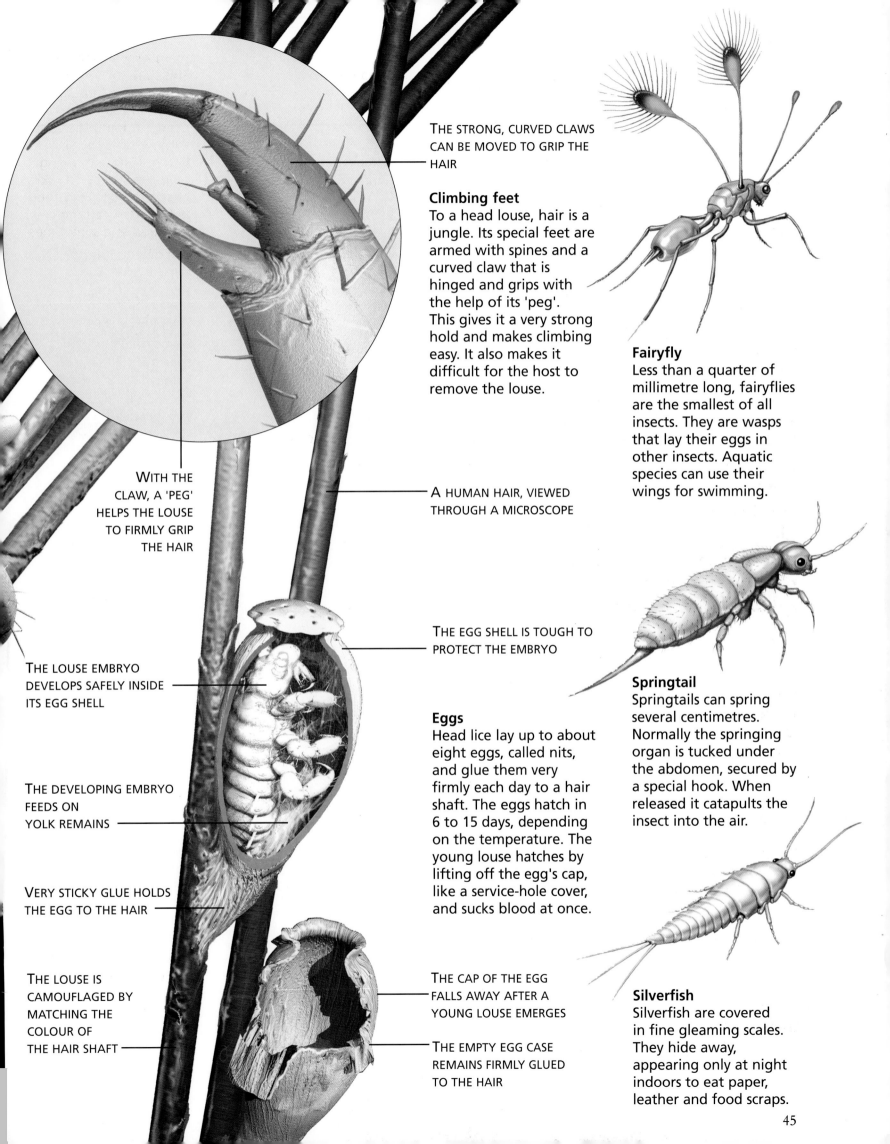

THE STRONG, CURVED CLAWS CAN BE MOVED TO GRIP THE HAIR

**Climbing feet**
To a head louse, hair is a jungle. Its special feet are armed with spines and a curved claw that is hinged and grips with the help of its 'peg'. This gives it a very strong hold and makes climbing easy. It also makes it difficult for the host to remove the louse.

WITH THE CLAW, A 'PEG' HELPS THE LOUSE TO FIRMLY GRIP THE HAIR

A HUMAN HAIR, VIEWED THROUGH A MICROSCOPE

THE LOUSE EMBRYO DEVELOPS SAFELY INSIDE ITS EGG SHELL

THE EGG SHELL IS TOUGH TO PROTECT THE EMBRYO

THE DEVELOPING EMBRYO FEEDS ON YOLK REMAINS

**Eggs**
Head lice lay up to about eight eggs, called nits, and glue them very firmly each day to a hair shaft. The eggs hatch in 6 to 15 days, depending on the temperature. The young louse hatches by lifting off the egg's cap, like a service-hole cover, and sucks blood at once.

VERY STICKY GLUE HOLDS THE EGG TO THE HAIR

THE LOUSE IS CAMOUFLAGED BY MATCHING THE COLOUR OF THE HAIR SHAFT

THE CAP OF THE EGG FALLS AWAY AFTER A YOUNG LOUSE EMERGES

THE EMPTY EGG CASE REMAINS FIRMLY GLUED TO THE HAIR

**Fairyfly**
Less than a quarter of millimetre long, fairyflies are the smallest of all insects. They are wasps that lay their eggs in other insects. Aquatic species can use their wings for swimming.

**Springtail**
Springtails can spring several centimetres. Normally the springing organ is tucked under the abdomen, secured by a special hook. When released it catapults the insect into the air.

**Silverfish**
Silverfish are covered in fine gleaming scales. They hide away, appearing only at night indoors to eat paper, leather and food scraps.

# Index

**A**
abdomen 6–9, 15
antennae 6, 8, 12–13, 17, 23, 25, 27, 44
ant lions 42
ants 17, 32–3, 36, 37, 42
ants' nests 32–3, 36, 37, 42
anus 22, 23, 24
aphids 32
armour plating 6, 8–9

**B**
bees 18, 22
bees' nests 34–5
beetles 8–12, 14, 17, 20, 18–19, 26–7, 38, 40, 42, 43
blood 6, 22–5, 30, 44
bombardier beetles 18–19
brain 6, 7, 8, 10, 11, 13
breathing 6, 7
bugs 37, 38
bush crickets 22
butterflies 14, 20, 22, 29, 30, 36, 37, 40

**C**
caecae 23
camouflage 16, 18, 20, 36
caterpillars 18, 21, 28, 30, 31, 32, 42
chafer beetles 8
chemicals 18, 19, 26, 34
chrysalis (pupa) 30–33, 35, 38
cicadas 26
claws 9, 16, 24, 27, 45
cockchafer beetles 12
cockroaches 22–3, 29
colon 22
colour 11, 18, 20–21
crickets 22, 42
crop 6, 23, 25
cuticle 6–9, 13, 14, 18, 20, 30, 42

**D**
damselflies 11
darkling beetles 42, 43
desert insects 42–3
digestion 6, 7, 22–3, 24

dragonflies 12, 14, 39
dune crickets 42
dung beetles 43

**E**
eardrums 7
earwigs 12
eggs 12, 24, 26–30, 32–5, 42, 43, 45
epidermis 9
excretion 7, 19
exoskeleton 6, 8, 9, 24
eyes 6, 8, 10–11, 16, 17, 18, 44

**F**
fairyflies 45
feelers see antennae
feet 9, 13, 42
fertilization 27, 28, 29, 34
fleas 24–5
flies 10, 11, 14
flowers 11, 17
flying 14–15
food 6, 7, 22–3, 24, 32–5

**G**
galls 40, 41
gizzard 6, 22, 23
glow worms 26
grasshoppers 7, 36, 43
great diving beetles 38
gut 22, 23, 24, 25

**H**
hatching 30
head 6, 8, 16, 17
head lice 44–5
heart 6, 44
hinges 9
honey 33, 34, 35
honeybees 34–35
houseflies 22
hunting 16–17

**I**
ileum 22
intestines 7, 19, 44

**J**
jaws (mandibles) 6, 8, 16, 17, 18, 25, 39, 42

jewel wasps 43
joints 9, 14

**L**
lacewings 29, 40
ladybirds 41
larvae 32, 33, 34, 37, 38–9, 40, 41, 43
leaf insects 37
legs 6–9, 15–18, 21, 24, 44
locusts 6–7, 43
longhorn beetles 26–27

**M**
mandibles see jaws
mantids 16–17, 36
mating 26–7, 32
maxilla 8
mayflies 38
microscopic life 44–5
mosquitoes 22, 38
moths 12, 18, 26, 40, 41
moulting 30, 31
mouth 6, 8, 11, 22
muscles 8, 9, 14, 17, 19, 25

**N**
nectar 34
nerve cells 7, 10
nymphs 38, 39

**O**
ocelli 10
oesophagus 22, 25
ommatidia 10, 11
oocytes 28, 29
optic nerves 11
ovaries 26, 27, 28

**P**
parasites 24–5
poison 18, 36, 37
pollen 34, 35
pond skaters 39
praying mantids 16–17
pupa see chrysalis

**R**
rainforests 38–9
rectum 7, 19, 22, 24, 25
rhabdom 10

**S**
saliva 22, 23, 25
sawflies 12, 29, 41
scales 21
segments 8
self-defence 18–19
sense organs 8, 12
sensory cells 13
sensory pegs 13
shield bugs 37
silverfish 45
sperm 24, 26, 27, 28
spines 18, 36
springtails 12, 39, 45
stag beetles 17
stick insects 21, 29
sting 18, 42

**T**
tarsus 9
taste hairs 23
termites 12, 18, 37
testes 26, 27
thorax 8, 14, 15, 17, 22
thornbugs 36
tiger beetles 17, 42
trachea 6, 44
tree hoppers 36

**U**
uterus 26, 27

**V**
vagina 24

**W**
waggle dance 35
wasps 12, 14–15, 42, 43, 45
waste 22, 23
water boatmen 39
water insects 38–9
water scorpions 29
weevils 12, 40
whirligig beetles 10, 11, 38
wings 7, 8, 9, 14–15, 16, 20, 21, 30
woodland life 40–41

**Z**
zygotes 29